JERRY THOME

Jackson Hole, Wyoming Travel Guide 2023-2024

Where the Wild West meets Modern Comfort

Contents

Foreword

I have to admit that Jackson Hole, Wyoming ought to be at the top of your list if you enjoy the great outdoors and are searching for a place that is both breathtaking and exhilarating. I'll tell you why you should definitely travel to Jackson Hole because, believe me, I've been there and it's an amazing place.

Let's talk about the Tetons first and foremost. These mountains are very amazing to behold. Their magnificence makes you feel humbled as you stand in their shadow. For those who love the outdoors, Grand Teton National Park is a playground. The park boasts immaculate lakes, stunning mountain scenery, and a network of trails suitable for all skill levels, from easy strollers to experienced hikers.

Suppose you are hiking on a trail that leads to Hidden Falls or Inspiration Point. The trip itself is just as important as the destination. You are surrounded by the sound of nature and the crisp smell of pine. If you're lucky, you might be able to see some elk or moose grazing close by. I assure you that those mountains possess a unique kind of charm.

These days, discussing Jackson Hole would be incomplete without bringing up Yellowstone National Park. It's similar to getting astounding natural beauty for half the price. Only a short drive away is Yellowstone, the first national park in the world. This is where you will see bubbling mud pots that transport you to another planet, multicolored hot springs that resemble other landscapes, and geysers that blast hot water into the sky.

And there's Old Faithful, the world's most renowned geyser, I believe. It's truly a show to watch as it erupts almost exactly as planned. The power of nature is captivating when it is observed in action.

Remembering the animals is also important. Grizzly bears, wolves, bison, and many other animals can be found in Yellowstone. Because of the amazing species that may be seen there, the Lamar Valley is frequently referred to as the "Serengeti of North America". It is similar to having your own National Geographic documentary.

The nice thing about Jackson Hole is that it's a year-round

destination. Every season brings something different.

It's a hiker's dream come true in the spring, when the snow melts and the wildflowers blossom. The wildlife is especially active, and you may explore the parks without the summertime throng.

Summertime is about having adventures. Hiking, riding, and exploring are all made possible by the long, warm days. In addition, there are numerous outdoor celebrations and activities. One unforgettable event that you shouldn't miss is white-water rafting on the Snake River.

Fall has such beauty. The parks have an entirely different appearance when the leaves change to stunning tones of crimson and gold. A great time to see wildlife because the creatures are getting ready for winter.

Jackson Hole turns into a wintry paradise in the winter. The hills are ideal for snowboarding and skiing. You may relax with a cup of hot cocoa by a roaring fire while taking in the town's glittering lights. It is quite magical.

Okay, so let's discuss the town of Jackson specifically. It has a distinctly western feel. The town square's antler arches, which encircle it, somehow feel so distinctive. It has a Wild West vibe thanks to the boardwalks and wooden buildings, and there are lots of stores, galleries, and eateries to discover.

Make sure to stop by the Million Dollar Cowboy Bar, which is akin to entering a vintage Western film. You may enjoy live country music while sitting in authentic saddle-shaped barstools. Here, you may relax and experience the thrill of being a real cowboy or cowgirl.

However, Jackson Hole isn't only about wildness and cowboys. Here, the artistic scene is also flourishing. There are art galleries that display everything from modern to traditional western artwork. From live music to ballet, the Center for the Arts serves as a central location for cultural activities and performances. It combines the best qualities of both worlds, creative flare and natural beauty.

Don't worry if you're bringing the whole family; there will be plenty to occupy the children. Bring them to the Jackson Hole Rodeo to experience authentic cowboy culture. Hikes suitable for families, animal safaris, and even kid-friendly cowboy cookouts are available.

And Jackson Hole provides everything you need for a romantic getaway. Just picture yourself curled up in a log cabin overlooking the Tetons. Together, you can enjoy romantic horseback rides, exclusive sleigh rides, or just a candlelit meal at one of the town's cozy eateries. It's a romantic destination for two people.

I must admit, there's something unique about eco-friendly vacation in Jackson Hole. The inhabitants take great care in maintaining this gorgeous landscape. Farm-to-table dining options, environmentally friendly tours, and a genuine awareness of the environment are all there. Here, you can enjoy the wonders of nature with the knowledge that you are contributing to their preservation.

And you know something? Few places have the ability to make you feel as alive and connected to the world as this one, with its breathtaking scenery, plethora of outdoor activities, and lively culture.

So, are you prepared to put on your hiking boots, pack your bags, and travel to Jackson Hole? The mountains are calling, my friend, and I can assure you that this will be an unforgettable journey. The opportunity to witness Jackson Hole's untamed beauty is waiting for you; don't pass it up.

Preface

Tucked up in the shadow of the Rocky Mountains, Jackson Hole is in the northwest region of Wyoming. Its location puts it in the middle of some of the most breathtaking and untamed landscapes in the country. The Rocky Mountains, often known as the "Rockies," originate in British Columbia, Canada, and descend all the way to New Mexico. And Jackson Hole is a unique location within this enormous range.

Let's now discuss Jackson Hole itself. Despite the name, it's a valley rather than a hole in the ground. What a valley that is, too! The Teton Range, one of the tallest peaks in the Rockies, encircles the valley. The Teton Mountains are renowned for their sharp, sky-piercing peaks covered in snow. They give the valley a breathtaking backdrop that is impossible to describe, exuding inspiration and a sense of grandeur.

Wyoming's tallest peaks are found in the Teton Range. The tallest of them all, Grand Teton, is situated 4,198 meters (13,770 feet) above sea level. It's a sight to behold—imposing and uplifting. Other noteworthy peaks in the range are Teewinot and Mount Owen.

Jackson Hole's geology is similarly fascinating. Millions of years of geological processes were required to develop the valley itself. One of the biggest almost intact temperate ecosystems on Earth, the Greater Yellowstone Ecosystem, includes it. From the untamed terrain of the Tetons to the geysers in Yellowstone, the country is peppered with reminders of its volcanic past.

Not to be overlooked while discussing geysers are the remarkable geological features seen in the neighboring Yellowstone National Park. The world-famous geyser Old Faithful is renowned for its beautifully timed outbursts, which blast steam and hot water skyward with amazing regularity. In addition, the park is home to geothermal wonders that demonstrate the activity occurring beneath the Earth's surface, such as bubbling mud pots and multicolored hot springs.

In Jackson Hole's geography, water is a major force. The Snake River flows through the valley, its source in the Tetons. This river is essential, maintaining the region's unique environment in addition to offering breathtaking views. Water-based recreation is prevalent there, ranging from serene float tours to heart-pounding white-water rafting.

Many glacial lakes, such as Grand Teton National Park's Jackson Lake and Jenny Lake, are another boon to Jackson Hole. Some of the most recognizable and picturesque views in the area are produced by the reflection of the Tetons' high peaks in these pure, clear lakes. Not only are they picturesque, but they're also great for fishing, kayaking, and paddleboarding.

It's incredible how diverse Jackson Hole's geography is. There are many different types of habitats in the valley itself, ranging from lush woods to alpine meadows. A distinct variety of plants and wildlife can be found in each area. In a matter of minutes, you can go from strolling through deep forests of pine and fir to exploring plains covered in sagebrush.

And the fauna! There are a plethora of animals in this area. It's typical to see bison, elk, deer, and moose in the valley and the neighboring parks. In the more isolated regions, black and grizzly bears can be found. Of course, there are also the mysterious gray wolves, who were just brought back to the area and are experiencing a renaissance.

Jackson Hole enjoys all four seasons, with each bringing with it unique and striking alterations to the local topography. When the snow melts and the wildflowers blossom, spring is a season of rebirth. The scenery changes from a stark white world to a riot of color, and the air is filled with the aroma of wildflowers in bloom.

Summertime offers a wide range of events. The lengthy, balmy days are ideal for exploration, riding, and hiking. A variety of festivals and outdoor events that make the most of the nice weather are also available.

Autumn is a beautiful season. Aspen and cottonwood trees display striking hues of gold and red on their leaves. The parks appear completely different and the crisp air is revitalizing. As animals get ready for the winter, it's also an excellent time to see wildlife.

Then winter arrives, blanketing the surroundings in a layer of snow. A winter paradise emerges at Jackson Hole. The Jackson

Hole Mountain Resort's slopes come alive with skiers and snowboarders in search of new snow. Jackson itself transforms into a charming, glistening sanctuary where you may sip hot chocolate by the fire and become comfy.

The ecological significance of Jackson Hole is what makes it so remarkable. The area is a part of the Greater Yellowstone Ecosystem, which is frequently cited as one of the temperate zone's last sizable, relatively intact ecosystems. As a result, wildlife is able to move freely around the area and the centuries-old interactions between different species and their ecosystems are maintained.

Here, there is a strong devotion to environmental preservation. Sustainable travel is a way of life, not merely a fashion. There are eco-friendly tour operators, farm-to-table dining establishments, and a sincere appreciation for the natural environment.

I

Planning Your Trip

1

When to Visit

Tenton Range at Winter

Selecting the optimum time to visit Jackson Hole, Wyoming, is like picking the key that will open the door to your perfect adventure in this breathtaking area. All year long, Jackson Hole provides a variety of experiences, with each season revealing its own allure and distinct charm. The activities you can do, the weather you'll encounter, and the general atmosphere you'll feel will all depend on when you come. To assist you in choosing the right time to start your Jackson Hole adventure, let's examine each season.

Spring: from April until June

In Jackson Hole, springtime is a season of renewal with a revitalizing and enchanted air. Springtime may be your best season if you're fascinated by the appearance of fresh life, blossoming wildflowers, and tranquil scenery.

The valley comes alive in the springtime with a flurry of wild-flowers. Jackson Hole transforms into a rainbow of hues, when the meadows are covered in lupines, Indian paintbrush, and other wildflowers. There are many of opportunities for beautiful photos and leisurely walks.

The springtime is when wildlife is most active. Moose, bison, and elk all become more active as they leave their wintering grounds. The presence of migrating birds returning to the area is another delight for birdwatchers.

The shoulder season, which includes spring, is when fewer people travel. Since there won't be as many people on the hiking trails and parks, you'll have more private time to spend exploring in solitude.

The right environment for white-water rafting is created by rivers surging due to the melting snow, which appeals to thrill-seekers. You can go on thrilling white-water rafting excursions against the breathtaking backdrop of the mountains.

Summertime, (from June to August)

Jackson Hole's best season is summer, when you may enjoy a wide range of outdoor activities amid pleasant weather and long days. Summertime is ideal for visiting if you want exciting outdoor activities and cultural events.

Hiking, riding, and outdoor exploration are all made possible by the long days and mild summertime. There are routes to fit every skill level, whether you're an experienced hiker or just a casual stroller.

For those who love animals, summer is the best season. It is a fantastic chance to see elk, deer, and other wildlife in their native settings because animals are out and about and easily visible.

The immaculate lakes of Jackson Hole, such as Jenny Lake and Jackson Lake, provide fantastic opportunities for boating, kayaking, and paddleboarding. Enjoy the stunning scenery of the Tetons while you take in the beauty of the lakes.

Summer is a season full of festivals and cultural activities. You can choose from a wide range of leisure activities, such as music festivals and art exhibitions. Discover the culture of the area and take in the variety of events going on.

Long daylight hours during the summer let you make the most of your outside experiences. Without having to worry about daylight dying out, you can explore hiking trails, visit national parks, and partake in a variety of activities.

Autumn: (September through November)

Fall is the best time to visit Jackson Hole if you're drawn to the stunning fall foliage, lower temperatures, and the opportunity to see wildlife during its seasonal migrations.

Aspen and cottonwood trees convert into a vivid tapestry of gold and crimson in the fall, bringing with them a breathtaking shift of the surroundings. Photographers love this time of year because it's when the landscapes are at their most picturesque.

Many animals migrate to lower elevations in the fall in preparation for the winter. It's the finest season for wildlife aficionados because it's when you can see the most bears, elk, moose, and other species.

Fall offers more comfortable outdoor activities like hiking and wildlife viewing because of the lower temperatures. It's a serene season devoid of summer's searing heat.

Since fall is regarded as the shoulder season, there won't be as many travelers there. As a result, visiting national parks and their environs is more tranquil and personal.

Winter (December - March) Winter at Jackson Hole is a dream come true for everyone who is enchanted by the enchantment of a snow-covered landscape. This is the perfect season if you want to ski or snowboard, prefer the concept of warm winter surroundings, and enjoy seeing wildlife against a snowy backdrop.

The world-famous Jackson Hole Mountain Resort draws dedicated skiers and snowboarders from all around the world with its difficult terrain and deep powder. An excursion in winter sports is ideal right now.

The area is transformed into a beautiful winter wonderland in an amazing way. A charming and enchanting ambiance is created by the new snow covering towns, national parks, and mountain slopes.

Jackson Hole's communities exude a warm atmosphere filled with hot cocoa, crackling fires, and twinkling lights. With possibilities like private sleigh rides and cozy dinners, it's the perfect time of year for romantic getaways.

There are plenty of possibilities to see wildlife during the winter. Against the snowy backdrop, bison, elk, and other animals are commonly sighted. A safari in the winter brings remarkable and unusual wildlife encounters.

Those looking for something new and exciting to do can go dog sledding and snowmobiling throughout the winter, which makes for an exciting and unforgettable experience.

When you visit Jackson Hole will depend on your interests, preferences, and the kind of experience that you are looking for. Jackson Hole provides an enthralling experience in every season, whether you're captivated by the rebirth of spring, the adventure of summer, the brilliant hues of fall, or the charming snowfall of winter. Think about what you want and start your Jackson Hole adventure when it's most convenient for you.

2

How to Get There

S tep one in starting your journey through this breath-taking area is to go to Jackson Hole. Grand Teton and Yellowstone, two well-known national parks, are close to Jackson Hole, which is well-known for its outdoor activities and scenic surroundings. This chapter will assist you in finding your way to Jackson Hole whether you're traveling by car, plane, or any other mode of transportation.

By Air:

Jackson Hole Airport (JAC) is the most convenient location to fly into when visiting Jackson Hole. The town of Jackson is only ten minutes away from this airport, which is the only commercial airfield inside Grand Teton National Park.

Jackson Hole Airport is well-connected to major American cities. Direct flights from major locations like Denver, Salt Lake City, Dallas/Fort Worth, and Chicago are available to JAC. Also, nonstop flights are available from other major cities at the busiest times of the year.

Connecting flights are an option if there are no direct flights available to Jackson Hole. Jackson Hole is accessible via connecting flights from major airports such as Salt Lake City International Airport (SLC) and Denver International Airport (DEN). Additionally, they have excellent connections to other cities.

You'll discover a number of car rental companies at Jackson Hole Airport once you arrive. A common option is to rent a car, particularly if you want to see the area at your own speed. Jackson's town is only a short, picturesque drive from the airport.

If you would rather not rent a car, the airport offers cabs and shuttle services. It is advisable to inquire with your accomodation about their complimentary shuttle services to and from the airport, as many places in Jackson provide these.

Via Road:

Traveling to Jackson Hole by car can be a beautiful and unique experience if you like doing road trips or are traveling from a neighboring area.

You can travel the stunning and historic U.S. Route 89 if you're traveling from Salt Lake City, Utah. There are amazing views while driving through the Bridger-Teton National Forest. Depending on the state of the roads, the trip takes between four and five hours.

U.S. Route 191 South can be taken by visitors from Montana or Yellowstone National Park. From the southern entrance of the park, the drive takes two to three hours, going through Grand

Teton National Park.

Travelers or residents of Idaho may drive from Idaho Falls along U.S. Route 26/89/189. Two to three hours are spent driving.

You can explore the area more freely if you rent a car. You can pick up your vehicle at the airport or neighborhood rental agencies. Major car rental firms have offices in Jackson.

By Bus:
   There are a few choices accessible to visitors who wish to get to Jackson Hole by bus. Utilizing these services is an economical and sustainable approach to travel to the area.

Jackson's public bus system is called Southern Teton Area Rapid Transit, or START. It provides routes around Jackson, including Teton Village, and within the town itself. It's an affordable method of exploring the area.

Jackson Hole is connected to neighboring cities by intercity bus services such as Greyhound and Salt Lake Express. Travelers on a tight budget will find these buses to be a practical alternative. They can drop you off at important Jackson locations and frequently have planned routes.

Additionally, private shuttle companies provide routes that link Jackson Hole to neighboring airports and cities. Their transportation service is both direct and comfortable.

By Train:
   Although Jackson Hole doesn't have a train station, you can

take the train to Idaho Falls, Idaho, a nearby town that is about two hours' drive from Jackson. This region is served by the picturesque California Zephyr route on Amtrak. To get to Jackson Hole from Idaho Falls, you can take a bus, rent a car, or utilize other modes of transportation.

By Bicycle:

A network of picturesque bike routes and roads is available in Jackson Hole for those who enjoy riding and adventure. It's a biker's paradise with stunning natural scenery and well-kept tracks. A bike ride to Jackson Hole is a great option if you're seeking an eco-friendly and athletic mode of transportation. You are welcome to bring your own bicycle or rent one from the area.

Navigating Jackson Hole

You'll need to know how to move around after you get to Jackson Hole so you can move about and explore the area. These are some choices:

1. **Rental Cars**: Hiring a car is a common way to go around the area at your own speed. Jackson Hole Airport and the municipality of Jackson are home to major vehicle rental firms.

2. **START Bus:** Jackson and the neighboring communities can access reasonably priced public transportation through the START Bus system. If you wish to go locally and are staying in the town, it's a convenient alternative.

3. **Shuttle Services**: Private shuttle services are available within Jackson Hole and can provide a practical means of getting to

neighboring events or sites.

4. **Biking**: If you intend to remain in Jackson Hole, riding a bike is a terrific way to see the town. Bikes are provided for free by many lodging establishments, and there are businesses where you can rent bikes.

5. **Walking**: Jackson's town is walkable, with a lot of sights, stores, and eateries in close proximity. The best way to experience the vibe of the town is to explore on foot.

3

What to Pack

P acking for a trip to Jackson Hole, Wyoming, demands considerable attention, as the region's unique temperature and vast selection of outdoor activities call for a well-thought-out packing list. Whether you're traveling during the summer or winter, or simply planning for a range of excursions, this chapter will help you prepare for your Jackson Hole journey.

Before we go into packing specifics, it's necessary to understand the climate in Jackson Hole, as this will be a major element in determining what to carry. Jackson Hole experiences four distinct seasons, each with its unique weather patterns:

1. **Spring (April to June):** Spring in Jackson Hole is a transitional season distinguished by steadily increasing temperatures. Early spring can still be extremely frigid, with occasional snow showers, while late spring sees milder temperatures and the appearance of wildflowers.

2. **Summer (June to August)**: Summer is the warmest season, with moderate daytime temperatures and colder evenings. Days can range from moderate to hot, and it's vital to be prepared for sunshine and the risk of infrequent afternoon thunderstorms.

3. **Fall (September to November)**: Fall is marked by crisp, chilly weather and spectacular beauty as the leaves change color. Days can still be rather pleasant, but nights grow frigid. Snowfall can occur towards the conclusion of the season.

4. **Winter (December to March)**: Winter in Jackson Hole is cold, with sub-freezing temperatures and regular snowfall. It's a snowy wonderland, making it a prime time for winter sports fans.

Now that we have a handle of the region's environment, let's consider what to pack for your Jackson Hole journey, bearing in mind the many seasons and activities you might want to enjoy.

1. **Clothing:** -
   Summer: Light, breathable clothing for daytime activities. Don't forget a swimsuit if you wish to enjoy the region's lakes and rivers. Be prepared for chilly evenings with a light jacket or sweater.

- Spring: Layered clothing for unpredictable weather. Include a waterproof and windproof jacket, as spring can bring unpredictable showers and frigid gusts.

- Fall: Pack layers for cool days and chilly evenings. A mid-weight jacket or coat is needed. Consider taking a scarf, gloves, and a warm cap.

- Winter: Warm, insulated gear is necessary. This comprises a large winter coat, waterproof and insulated boots, thermal layers, gloves, a scarf, and a beanie. Don't forget your ski or snowboard gear if you plan to hit the slopes.

2. **Footwear:** -
   Summer: Comfortable hiking shoes, sandals for water sports, and casual shoes for town tours.

- Spring and Fall: Waterproof hiking boots with good traction for exploring the changing landscapes and unexpected weather.

- Winter: Insulated and waterproof snow boots for snowy circumstances. Make sure they are warm and comfy for winter sports.

3. **Accessories**: -
   Sun Protection: Sunglasses, a wide-brimmed hat, and sunscreen are vital, especially during the bright summer months.

- Winter Gear: If you're visiting during the winter, pack skiing or snowboarding gear, including goggles, a helmet, and warm mittens.

4. Outdoor Gear: - Backpack: A daypack is useful for transporting basics, such as water, snacks, and additional layers, during outdoor trips.

- Hiking Gear: If you plan on hiking, make sure to carry a good-quality backpack, a route map, a water bottle, and strong hiking poles.

- Water Gear: If you'll be spending time on the lakes and rivers, consider carrying kayaking or paddleboarding gear, or at the absolute least, a swimsuit.

- Camping Gear: For campers, add a tent, sleeping bag, and camping equipment suitable for the season. Check the local regulations and standards.

5. **Electronics & Gadgets:** - Camera: Jackson Hole is a heaven for photographers. Bring your camera or smartphone with a good camera to capture the breathtaking landscapes.

- Binoculars: If you're interested in wildlife observation, a pair of binoculars is a wonderful addition to your packing list.

- Power Bank: Ensure you have a power bank to keep your electronics charged, especially if you're going to be on lengthy walks or camping vacations.

- Adapters: Depending on your region, you may require plug adapters to charge your devices.

6. **Miscellaneous Items**: - First Aid Kit: It's recommended to take a basic first-aid kit, especially if you're going to be distant from medical services.

- Medications: If you require any prescription medications, bring a enough supply and a copy of your prescription.

- Maps and Guidebooks: Having physical maps and guidebooks (like the one you're reading) might be beneficial for navigating the area, especially if you'll be exploring rural places.

- Reusable Water Bottle: Staying hydrated is vital, and carrying a reusable water bottle is an eco-friendly and convenient way to do so.

- Cash and Cards: While most places in Jackson Hole accept credit cards, it's a good idea to carry some cash for smaller shops or outdoor activities.

- Ziplock Bags: These can be great for storing snacks, preserving your devices from dampness, and keeping things organized.

7. **Winter Sports Gear**: If you're visiting Jackson Hole in the winter to experience the region's famed skiing and snowboarding, make sure to pack your winter sports gear, including:

- Skis or snowboard - Ski boots or snowboard boots
    - Ski/snowboard bindings
    - Warm, moisture-wicking base layers
    - Ski/snowboard jacket and pants
    - Snow gloves or mittens
    - Ski/snowboard helmet - Goggles
    - Neck gaiter or balaclava - Hand and foot warmers

8. **Travel Documents**:
    - Passport or driver's license
    - Travel insurance information - Hotel reservations - Flight itineraries - Any required licenses for activities like camping or

fishing

9. **Leave No Trace:** As you prepare to enjoy the natural splendor of Jackson Hole, remember the ideals of Leave No Trace. This includes packing out any waste and following standards for responsible outdoor activities.

II

Exploring the Towns

4

Jackson Town

J ackson Hole, Wyoming, is a place of outstanding natural beauty, attracting adventurers, nature enthusiasts, and travelers from all corners of the globe. And at the center of this gorgeous valley lies a charming hamlet that serves as the perfect blend of Western authenticity and modern comforts: Jackson hamlet.

Before we delve into the various activities and experiences that Jackson Town provides today, it's vital to grasp the town's historical significance and rich legacy. The town's history may be traced back to the early 19th century when it was initially formed as a fur trade center. It later blossomed into a thriving village centered around livestock, timber, and, eventually, tourism.

The town's rustic beauty and historic buildings, such as the

Wort Hotel and the Million Dollar Cowboy Bar, pay respect to its Wild West past. A remarkable feature of the town square is the unique elk antler arches, made from the shed antlers of the local elk herd. These arches highlight the deep link between Jackson Town and the surrounding natural surroundings.

The town square, sometimes referred to as George Washington Memorial Park, acts as a hive of activity and the town's social focal point. Bordered by distinctive boutiques, art galleries, restaurants, and pubs, it's a spot where locals and visitors come to absorb in the ambiance and energy that distinguishes Jackson Town.

The four elk antler arches that guard the corners of the plaza are not just photo-worthy icons but also a tribute to the town's devotion to preserve its past. In the summer, the town square provides the setting for the legendary Jackson Hole Shootout, a reenactment of Old West-style shootouts complete with cowboys, outlaws, and a lively crowd.

Jackson Town offers a shopping experience that perfectly compliments its artistic and cultural legacy. The town enjoys a lively arts culture, with various galleries showing the work of local and regional artists. From Western-inspired paintings that capture the soul of the American West to modern sculptures, the galleries provide a varied range of artistic interpretations.

If you're seeking souvenirs or unique presents, the town's stores provide a great choice of options. You may purchase locally produced jewelry, apparel, outdoor gear, and home decor, each with its distinct Western flavor. These shops provide the option to take a piece of Jackson Town's charm home with you.

Jackson Town is recognized for its unique gastronomic choices. A visit to this town provides a gourmet excursion that caters to every appetite. The local cuisine celebrates Western traditions and flavors, with bison, elk, and trout typically taking center stage.

The town's food scene caters to a broad variety of preferences. Fine dining establishments deliver exquisite, delicious dishes prepared from locally sourced ingredients. These restaurants offer a romantic environment and top-notch service, making them ideal for a memorable evening out.

For those wanting a more casual eating experience, Jackson Town features a range of bistros, diners, and family-friendly eateries. Don't miss the opportunity to sample favorites like chicken-fried steak or the legendary bison burger.

Cafes and bakeries provide a fantastic start to the day with freshly made coffee and pastries. As the sun sets, restaurants and breweries come alive, offering artisan beers, unusual cocktails, and a lively social environment.

Beyond its cultural and culinary offers, Jackson Town provides a gateway to outdoor excursions. It is conveniently positioned to allow quick access to Grand Teton National Park, an outdoor paradise noted for its beautiful peaks, clean lakes, and rich wildlife. The park offers an assortment of recreational options, including hiking, wildlife viewing, and water-based sports like boating and fishing.

For winter aficionados, Jackson Town is an ideal location for experiencing some of the best skiing and snowboarding in the United States. Jackson Hole Mountain Resort, situated just a short drive away, provides access to world-class slopes and snow. The town itself is characterized by a strong ski culture, with stores offering gear rentals and instruction for all ability levels.

Jackson Town is more than just a tourism attraction; it is a thriving community with a strong sense of togetherness. The town hosts many events throughout the year, providing residents and visitors with opportunity to join together and celebrate. From the weekly Town Square Shootout during the summer months to festive holiday celebrations in the winter, these activities reflect the local spirit and create a warm and welcome atmosphere.

5

Teton Village

Jackson Hole Mountain Resort

Teton Village, nestled at the base of the renowned Jackson Hole Mountain Resort in Wyoming, is a location that encapsulates the spirit of adventure, the allure of the great outdoors, and the grandeur of the Tetons.

This scenic alpine community is a hub for outdoor enthusiasts year-round, offering a diversity of activities and experiences that make it an unforgettable part of the Jackson Hole region.

Teton Village's crowning jewel is the Jackson Hole Mountain Resort. Known for its world-class skiing and snowboarding in the winter, as well as hiking and mountain biking in the summer, the resort serves as a year-round playground for those seeking epic adventure. Towering above the community, the craggy peaks of the Teton Range provide the perfect background for thrill-seekers and nature lovers alike.

For those who appreciate the rush of cold mountain air and the excitement of conquering snow-covered slopes, Teton Village in winter is a delight. The Jackson Hole Mountain Resort boasts approximately 2,500 acres of skiable terrain, making it one of the most vast ski slopes in North America. Its famed steep and hard courses have earned it a reputation as a destination for expert skiers and snowboarders.

The resort's state-of-the-art amenities, including the Aerial Tram and multiple chairlifts, offer convenient access to the slopes. Whether you're a seasoned powder hound or a newbie hitting the slopes for the first time, the resort provides training and programs for all levels of skill.

When the snow melts, Teton Village morphs into a summer playground. The neighboring mountains become a hiking and mountain biking heaven, with trails that weave through pristine alpine meadows and deep forests. The Teton Village region is the entryway to a myriad of outdoor excursions, from relaxing nature walks to demanding backcountry hikes.

One popular summer attraction is the Bridger Gondola, which lifts people to high alpine areas. From the peak, you can begin on walks that give amazing vistas of the Tetons and the surrounding countryside. For mountain bikers, the resort's slopes give thrilling descents and cross-country routes, and you can even put your bike aboard the gondola for an elevated start.

Teton Village's heart is a vibrant pedestrian village that offers an enticing blend of stores, restaurants, and bars. After a day of action, the village is the ideal spot to relax and unwind. Cozy up with a cup of hot cocoa, relish a big meal, or sip on a craft brew at one of the village's cafés. You'll find a range of food options, from casual and family-friendly to expensive dining experiences, many with magnificent mountain vistas.

As the sun sets, the community comes to life with après-ski and après-hike festivities. Live music and social gatherings are a common sight, creating the perfect atmosphere for exchanging stories and making new acquaintances.

Teton Village's proximity to Grand Teton National Park is a big appeal for visitors. The park, noted for its rough mountain landscapes, clean lakes, and plentiful animals, is just a short drive away. Some of the park's most iconic sights, including Jenny Lake and Cascade Canyon, are easily accessible from Teton Village. Hiking, wildlife viewing, and tranquil picnics by the lakeshore are popular activities for tourists wishing to appreciate the park's natural treasures.

Teton Village provides a variety of housing alternatives, from luxury resorts to intimate mountain cabins. The Jackson Hole Mountain Resort has magnificent hotels and residences that cater to guests seeking comfort and convenience. Many accommodations in the village offer ski-in/ski-out access, allowing you to hit the slopes or the trails right from your doorstep.

The service at Teton Village is recognized for its warmth and hospitality, ensuring that guests have a memorable and comfortable stay.

Teton Village doesn't slow down with the changing seasons. It hosts a wide array of events throughout the year, including music festivals, outdoor movie nights, and holiday celebrations. The village's events offer a chance to connect with the local community and immerse yourself in the region's culture.

6

Wilson

Wilson is a hidden gem that beckons visitors looking for a more tranquil and rustic getaway. It is located in the center of Jackson Hole, sheltered by the majestic Teton Range. While Jackson Hole is renowned for its adventure and vibrant towns, Wilson provides a slower tempo, a closer connection to nature, and a true look at the Old West charm that characterizes the area.

Wilson's past and the rich legacy of the American West are deeply entwined. With an emphasis on ranching and agricultural activities, the town was established in the late 1800s. The expansive lawns, undulating meadows, and sporadic horse-drawn carriages that you may come across on Wilson's small-town streets all bear witness to this heritage.

Many of the town's buildings still have their original, traditional Western architecture, giving the place a true Western feel. The surrounding wilderness, which offers a magnificent backdrop for outdoor activity, and Wilson's ranching heritage have created the city's culture.

The Snake River passes through Wilson, enhancing the town's allure and serving as a vital link in the surrounding ecology. Fly fishers can catch a variety of trout species in the clear, cool waters of this pristine creek, which is a well-known fly-fishing destination. When it comes to experiencing this well-liked activity, tourists often opt for guided fishing trips along the Snake River.

Rafting and floating trips along the Snake River are popular due to its breathtaking scenery. You can see creatures in their natural habitat, such as moose, eagles, and beavers, by taking leisurely floats along serene sections of the river.

Wilson is known for its tight-knit community, which is one of its key features. The town holds a range of activities and get-togethers that showcase the rich local culture. These events offer an opportunity to interact with the locals and become fully immersed in the history of the town, ranging from farmers' markets and community picnics to music festivals and art exhibitions.

Wilson residents embrace the town's reputation for hospitality and are well-known for their warm and inviting personalities. Whether they are taking part in a community event or are just chatting with a nice local at one of the town's businesses, visitors frequently have a sense of belonging.

Wilson provides a singular chance for art fans to discover regional originality. There are many art galleries and studios in the neighborhood that display the creations of regional artists. Explore a range of artistic works that encapsulate the spirit of the

American West and the breathtaking Teton scenery, including sculptures and paintings with a Western influence.

Additionally, the town is home to the well-known Stagecoach Bar. For many years, both locals and tourists have gathered at this historic venue, which features a wooden bar, live music, and dancing. It's a must-go if you want to take in a little bit of Western culture in a friendly and laid-back atmosphere.

There are lots of chances for outdoor excursions amid the untamed countryside that surrounds Wilson. Due to its proximity to Grand Teton National Park, the community has access to peaceful lakes, hiking trails, and animal viewing possibilities. The well-known Jenny Lake in the park is only a short drive away, and kayaking, paddleboarding, and picturesque boat cruises are all excellent in its pure waters.

For hiking, camping, and horseback riding, the adjacent Bridger-Teton National Forest offers a huge playground. With a wide variety of trails to choose from, explorers may get up close and personal with the Teton Range's breathtaking scenery.

Wilson's dining selections provide a pleasant taste of the West. Dishes that highlight the flavors of the area are served in local restaurants, with a focus on game meats such bison and elk. In the town, farm-to-table dining is popular and guarantees that the ingredients are fresh and sourced locally. The town's cafés and restaurants offer a warm, welcoming atmosphere for dining, with many of them situated against the breathtaking Tetons backdrop.

In Wilson, lodging options vary from charming bed & breakfasts to cozy cabins and guest ranches. With these choices, guests may take advantage of contemporary conveniences while fully embracing the tranquil ambiance of the town.

7

Moose

Jenny Lake

I n the center of the well-known Grand Teton National Park, Moose, Wyoming, is a charming community tucked away in the foothills of the Teton Range. With its stunning alpine lakes, wild and untamed scenery, and rough environment, this isolated village provides a genuine window into the raw and untamed splendor of the American West. Because of their location within Grand Teton National Park, moose, despite their modest population, have great historical significance. Moose were crucial to the park's creation, which took place in 1929 with the intention of safeguarding and preserving the Teton Range's natural splendor.

The town's past is entwined with outdoor leisure, farming, and ranching, evoking the pioneer spirit of the American West in its early years. The large numbers of moose that once roamed the region are the source of the word "moose." The town and the surrounding woods coexist peacefully, as the name suggests.

Moose now serves as the entrance to Grand Teton National Park, giving tourists a place to start their exploration of the park's majesty and the immense wilderness that characterizes the area.

One of the most prominent features of Moose is its center placement within Grand Teton National Park. With access to some of the park's most well-known features, it functions as a crucial intersection. For visitors wishing to experience the park's attractions, the visitor center and ranger station in Moose offer vital supplies, knowledge, and assistance.

Moose offers visitors spectacular views of the famous Grand Teton, one of the most identifiable peaks in the whole Rocky Mountain range. Standing tall above the town, this mountain provides as a constant reminder of the wild grandeur that envelops Moose.

Moose's position in the center of the Teton Range provides unmatched chances for outdoor experiences and a close relationship with the natural world. Numerous outdoor pursuits that provide a glimpse of the untamed splendor of the Tetons can be found in the vicinity.

Hikers and outdoor enthusiasts will find paradise in Moose. There is a vast network of hiking paths in Grand Teton National Park that may be customized to suit different hiking skill levels and tastes. There's a trail for everyone, from leisurely walks around lakeshores to strenuous hikes up mountains.

Trekkers can experience well-known paths such as Jenny Lake, Taggart Lake, and Cascade Canyon, each offering a special combination of wildlife encounters, tranquil lakeside settings, and mountain views. The paths surrounding Moose offer a close encounter with the natural landscapes of the Tetons, whether you're looking for a leisurely stroll or an intense climb.

fauna aficionados and photographers find Grand Teton National Park to be an ideal location due to its variety and abundant fauna. In addition to the frequently sighted moose, elk, deer, and bison, the park is home to grizzly and black bears, wolves, and elusive mountain lions.

A front-row perspective to this dynamic ecology is provided by Moose. There are many opportunities to photograph these moments when you see animals in their natural environments, which may be a captivating experience.

Respecting wildlife and keeping a safe distance from it is crucial to ensuring both the animals' safety and the continuation of their natural habits.

Within the national park, Moose offers camping opportunities for people looking for a more immersed experience. Campsites such as Jenny Lake and Gros Ventre provide an opportunity to sleep beneath the stars and awaken in the middle of unspoiled nature.

Backcountry exploration is an exciting alternative for people who enjoy being alone and have an adventurous spirit. Sightseeing and off-roading options abound for skilled hikers and mountaineers amid the park's extensive wildness. For backcountry excursions, the right equipment, permits, and safety measures are crucial.

One of Grand Teton National Park's most recognizable features, Jenny Lake, is conveniently located from Moose. Surrounded by towering peaks, thick forests, and peaceful shorelines, this glacial lake is glistening with clean water. Hiking the scenic walk that winds along the lake's shore is another way that visitors can explore the area. Boat excursions are also available across the lake.

Additionally, the Jenny Lake region is home to a visitor center that offers crucial details and perspectives on the natural history, geology, and ecological significance of the park.

Moose has always served as an inspiration for writers, photographers, and artists, even if the area's natural beauty takes center stage. Numerous pieces of literature, art, and photography have drawn inspiration from the serene surroundings of Moose and the untamed grandeur of the Tetons. The town's atmosphere, characterized by the majesty of the Tetons and the purity of nature, has long served as a source of creative inspiration.

Even though it's not a busy city, Moose has housing and food alternatives to meet the demands of tourists. For those looking for sophistication in the middle of the forest, Jenny Lake Lodge offers an opulent getaway. Fine food, cozy lodging, and the ideal fusion of comfort and nature are all on offer.

Colter Bay Village offers hotel alternatives such as cottages and camping for a more rustic experience. For those who have braved far into the woods, the park's food establishments provide filling meals.

8

Moran

Small and remote, Moran is tucked away at the northern end of Jackson Hole Valley and offers a unique entry point to the raw grandeur of the American West. It is surrounded by the unspoiled wilderness of Grand Teton National Park. Moran is a paradise for nature lovers, outdoor adventurers, and people looking for a close connection with the outdoors because of its closeness to the Tetons, wealth of wildlife, and rough terrain.

The history of Moran is closely linked to the area's ranching and farming traditions. Originally founded in the late 1800s, the town was a resting place for cattle ranchers and visitors, and its distinctive views of the Teton Range and homey atmosphere offered a warm and pleasant escape for those traveling through. Thomas "Broken Hand" Moran, an early fur trapper and adventurer who traveled through the area, is the source of the town's moniker.

The town's small-town feel and the surrounding scenery show

that Moran hasn't forgotten its Western heritage. The town's identity is still shaped by its historical significance and the part it played in the development of the area.

Being the entry point to Grand Teton National Park, Moran's location is one of its most distinctive qualities. Being close to the park's northern entrance makes it a convenient starting point for exploring its breathtaking scenery, untamed mountains, and varied ecosystems.

The striking Teton Range greets visitors at Moran and sets the mood for their trek into the heart of Grand Teton National Park. The park is renowned for its immaculate lakes, high peaks, and plethora of species, making it a veritable gold mine of scenic splendor.

The area around Moran is a natural playground for those who enjoy being outside. The town itself serves as the starting point for a variety of excursions and experiences that showcase the area's unspoiled natural settings.

There is a vast network of hiking routes in Grand Teton National Park, many of which are reachable from Moran. The park has paths for hikers of all skill levels, whether they are experienced backpackers searching for strenuous climbs or a family looking for a relaxing stroll through the natural environment.

Trails like Two Ocean Lake, Christian Pond, and Heron Pond are available for hikers to explore in Moran; each offers a different combination of peaceful lakeside settings, mountain views, and wildlife interactions. Because of Moran's position, guests can have a personalized tour of the area's natural beauties.

One of Moran's main draws for tourists is the park's diverse array of wildlife. Common sightings include bison, pronghorn, elk, moose, and deer. In addition, wolves, black bears, grizzly bears, and other elusive species are well-known for living in Grand Teton National Park.

Photographers flock to Moran because of the chance to get amazing shots of these amazing creatures in their native environments. For the safety of the animals as well as your own, you must respect them and keep a safe distance.

Those who wish to fully immerse themselves in the nature can camp within Moran's national park. Campgrounds with lakefront sites, starry sky, and quiet evenings in the outdoors, including Lizard Creek and Colter Bay, offer a tranquil getaway.

For seasoned hikers and mountaineers, exploring the wilderness is an exciting choice. Grand Teton National Park is home to large wilderness areas; visitors must be prepared with the right equipment, permits, and safety measures before entering these areas.

Jackson Lake, one of the biggest high-elevation lakes in the US, is conveniently close to Moran. Activities on the water are available at the lake, including kayaking, fishing, and boating. The Teton Range provide a striking background for Jackson Lake, making it a wonderful place for relaxing, swimming, and picnics.

The many bays and inlets of the lake can be explored by guests with the help of guided boat trips and rentals. When out on the lake in a boat, sightings of bald eagles, osprey, and ducks are not unusual.

Although Moran isn't a big city, it does have accommodations for travelers, including food and hotel. Situated on the banks of Jackson Lake, the Signal Mountain Lodge offers a variety of lodging options, ranging from contemporary lakeside rooms to rustic cabins. In addition, the lodge has eating areas where campers and hikers can enjoy filling meals.

Small restaurants, cafes, and businesses that serve tourists touring the area may be found all across the town of Moran. It's the perfect location to resupply and savor a hot lunch following an exciting day of exploration.

Moran has a sense of camaraderie and hospitality that is characteristic of small Western towns, even though it might not host big events. Locals and company owners are frequently delighted to provide guests advice, anecdotes, and insights.

Attending community activities, such farmers' markets and get-togethers, is a great opportunity to meet people and learn about the town's way of life. Moran has a timeless appeal that is demonstrated by its friendly and inviting ambiance.

9

Hoback Junction

This quaint village, which is situated where the Hoback and Snake Rivers converge, offers a special fusion of outdoor activity, scenic beauty, and the tranquil pace of country life. The history of Hoback Junction is rich in Wild West legend. The town takes its name from John Hoback, an early 19th-century explorer and trapper who traveled through the area. When the region was opened, it served as a resting place for settlers, fur trappers, and pioneers making their way through the wild West.

Hoback Junction's rural origins are deeply ingrained in its historical significance, and the town's ambiance still has traces of this legacy. Modern amenities have made their way here, but the spirit of the West—rugged individualism, self-sufficiency, and a connection to the land—remains.

The center of Jackson Hole is a highly sought-after location since Hoback Junction is not just a charming hamlet but also the starting point for an abundance of outdoor excursions.

For lovers of river experiences, the confluence of the Hoback and Snake Rivers is a paradise. Here, fly fishing is very popular because there are many different varieties of trout in the rivers. Casting a line into the region's pristine waters is the best way to connect with nature. Both novice and expert fisherman can take advantage of guided fishing trips.

Kayaking, canoeing, and paddleboarding are excellent options for anyone looking for a more relaxed river experience. The rivers' serene, unspoiled waters offer a picturesque backdrop for discovering the nearby flora and fauna.

Hoback Junction's close vicinity to the Caribou-Targhee National Forest and the Bridger-Teton National Forest provides access to an abundance of hiking and outdoor exploring opportunities. Hikers of all skill levels can choose from a wide variety of trails because to the area's untamed landscape, thick forests, and alpine meadows.

Deep within the forest is a natural thermal pool called Granite Hot Springs, which is a popular hiking destination. A relaxing dip in the beautiful natural surroundings of the hot springs after a tiring climb is the ideal way to decompress.

Hoback Junction is a little town, but it has a big feeling of community and belonging. The town's citizens and business owners uphold the ideals of the American West, creating a welcoming environment and a sense of neighborly solidarity. Hoback Junction is more than just a tourism destination; it's a location where one may immediately feel at home. Visitors are frequently greeted with open arms.

Local get-togethers and events, such festivals, farmers' markets, and community picnics, give locals and visitors a chance to interact, exchange tales, and become fully immersed in the town's culture. The spirit of community in the town really comes alive during these times.

Despite its modest size, Hoback Junction provides a range of housing and dining alternatives to meet the demands of visitors. There are several quaint cafés, restaurants, and eateries in the area that serve filling meals with a hint of regional flair. It's the perfect spot to have a hot supper following an exciting day outside.

10

Where to Stay

D eciding the perfect place to lay your head in Jackson Hole, Wyoming, is another vital part of planning your stay in this gorgeous region. From luxury resorts to small cabins, there's a vast choice of housing alternatives to fit any traveler's preferences and budget. Let's explore some of the housing possibilities in Jackson Hole, so you can choose the perfect spot to stay during your vacation.

1. Hotels and Resorts:

Jackson Hole offers a number of hotels and resorts that cater to diverse interests, from high luxury to more affordable lodgings. Here are a few significant options:

A Room in Amangani Hotel

- **Amangani**: Located on East Gros Ventre Butte, Amangani is a luxury resort that offers amazing views of the Teton Range. The resort has exquisite rooms and suites, a spa, and fine restaurants. It's a fantastic alternative for individuals seeking a luxurious experience. For more inquiries you can phone +1 307-734-7333. For real time directions from Jackson Hole to the hotel, click here:

    https://maps.app.goo.gl/5fpKaWzDAKs2UV1R8

Four Seasons Resort

- **Four Seasons Resort**: You'll find this Resort at 7680 Granite Loop Road, Teton Village. This well-known luxury brand has a presence in Jackson Hole, offering top-notch amenities, including a spa, restaurants, and a wide selection of outdoor activities. It's a terrific choice for people looking for a sumptuous escape. For more information phone +1 307-732-5000.

Click here for real time directions from Jackson Hole:

https://maps.app.goo.gl/AF5W74PZ8pXZMv8Q9

- **Hotel Jackson:** Located in the heart of Jackson, precisely at 120 Glenwood, St. Jackson, WY 83001, this boutique hotel mixes modern conveniences with a rustic, Western-inspired design. It's within walking distance of the town square, making it a convenient choice for exploring Jackson's food and retail options. The number to call for any further inquiries is +1 307-

733-2200.

As always, go here for real time directions from Jackson Hole:

https://maps.app.goo.gl/cKf3nWZa4CszDV1J7

Teton Mountain Lodge & Spa

- **Teton Mountain Lodge & Spa**: This mountain lodge in Teton Village offers a cozy alpine ambiance with a selection of lodging types and facilities like a spa, pool, and access to the Jackson Hole Mountain Resort. For more queries dial +1 307-201-6066.
   For real time instructions from Jackson, go here:
   https://maps.app.goo.gl/cJunnU9srtZLiujy8

- **Rustic Inns**:

   Jackson Hole also includes smaller inns and hotels that provide comfortable and budget-friendly accommodations. These options cater to guests seeking a more inexpensive stay while still enjoying the Jackson Hole experience. Let's investigate each of these inns in Jackson Hole, Wyoming, and what they have to offer:

Wyoming Inn

1. **Wyoming Inn of Jackson Hole**: The Wyoming Inn of Jackson Hole is an elegant inn that embodies the rustic character of the region while offering visitors with a magnificent experience. The inn is strategically positioned just a short drive from Jackson's town square, allowing easy access to dining, shopping, and local attractions. The Wyoming Inn offers big and comfortable accommodations with rustic yet sophisticated décor. Many rooms come with modern conveniences and some even offer fireplaces, balconies, and mountain views.

The inn's restaurant, The Whistling Grizzly, delivers superb Western cuisine, giving it a great venue to experience regional delicacies. Guests can take advantage of the fitness facility, outdoor hot tub, and beautifully landscaped grounds that provide a tranquil atmosphere for leisure. For more inquiries you can phone the inn at +1 307-734-0035. For real time instructions from Jackson hole, click here https://maps.app.goo.gl/xvHx7Xf srJbe5Zk49

Parkway Inn

2. **Parkway Inn**: Parkway Inn is a beautiful and family-friendly inn set in the center of Jackson. Parkway Inn's central position means you're just a short walk from Jackson's town square, where you can explore shops, galleries, and restaurants.

The inn offers pleasant and well-appointed rooms, including suites with sitting spaces and balconies. The warm, Western-inspired décor contributes to the friendly mood. Guests can enjoy a complimentary breakfast each morning, a terrific start to the day. Additionally, in the evenings, you can congregate for wine and cheese in the lobby. Parkway Inn includes an indoor pool and hot tub, as well as a lovely courtyard with a fireplace. Dial +1 307-733-3143 for more queries. For real time instructions from Jackson, go here: https://maps.app.goo.gl/pC 3hodda55i913P27

Elk Country Inn

3. Elk Country Inn: The Elk Country Inn is a comfortable and budget-friendly inn with a focus on offering guests with a cozy and convenient stay. This inn is located on the north end of Jackson, precisely at 480 W Pearl Ave, Jackson WY 83001, offering a quieter location while still affording convenient access to the town's attractions.

Elk Country Inn offers a variety of rooms, including kitchenette flats, making it an excellent choice for extended stays or families. The décor is modest and pleasant.

The inn has a hot tub and a fitness facility, providing relaxation and recreation choices. There's also a picnic area with barbecue grills for guests to utilize. The number to call for booking/inquiries is +1 307-733-2364. You can click here for realtime direction from Jackson; https://maps.app.goo.gl/CwK XbRDtznq5APnK9

Elk Refuge Inn

4. **Elk Refuge Inn:** The Elk Refuge Inn offers an intimate and budget-friendly choice for guests looking to stay near the National Elk Refuge.

As the name suggests, the inn is situated in close proximity to the National Elk Refuge and offers beautiful views of the Teton Range. It's a peaceful setting.

Rooms at Elk Refuge Inn are clean and pleasant, giving it a wonderful base for exploring the natural splendor of the region.

The inn includes a picnic area and barbecue grills, allowing visitors to enjoy meals and gatherings in a tranquil outdoor setting. The number to call for more inquiries is +1 307-200-

0981. For real time direction from Jackson click here: https://maps.app.goo.gl/P4ji23nGMkjSowdn9

Antler Inn

5. **Antler Inn:**

The Antler Inn is a budget-friendly inn situated in the heart of Jackson, offering convenient access to the town's attractions and activities. Antler Inn is located right on the town square of Jackson, providing easy access to restaurants, shops, galleries, and entertainment.

The inn offers comfortable rooms with a range of bed configurations to accommodate various group sizes. Rooms are modest but provide all the required conveniences for a nice stay.

While it's a more budget-conscious option, Antler Inn provides practical amenities, such as a hot tub and complimentary continental breakfast. The number to call for booking/inquiries is +1 307-733-2535.

For realtime directions from Jackson click here: For the best route in current traffic visit https://maps.app.goo.gl/cW4zd7te vq5rrnaAA

Bentwood Inn

7. **Bentwood Inn:**

The Bentwood Inn is an upscale bed and breakfast that offers a cozy and elegant mountain lodge experience. The inn is located just a short drive from Jackson, nestled in the serene Teton Village. This location provides easy access to outdoor activities and natural beauty. Bentwood Inn features beautifully decorated rooms and cabins with luxurious amenities. Some rooms have fireplaces and private decks with stunning mountain views.

Guests can enjoy a gourmet breakfast and evening appetizers during their stay, adding to the delightful experience.

The inn boasts a lovely outdoor hot tub and access to nearby hiking and biking trails. It's a great choice for a romantic getaway or a peaceful retreat. And yes, you can come with your kids. You can reach the inn at +1 307-739-1411. https://maps.app.goo.gl/RxyFLpDg3UgAC5P96

A room in Bentwood Inn

A room in Hampton Inn

8. **Hampton Inn:**

The Hampton Inn in Jackson offers comfortable and convenient accommodations with a focus on providing a pleasant and hassle-free stay. The inn is situated in Jackson, making it easy to access the town's attractions, dining, and shopping options. Hampton Inn provides well-appointed rooms with modern amenities, ensuring a comfortable stay for both leisure and business travelers. Guests can enjoy complimentary breakfast, a fitness center, and a heated indoor pool, offering relaxation and recreation options. For more inquiries dial +1 307-733-0033. For realtime direction from Jackson Hole, click here: https://maps.app.goo.gl/GiQZadKvP2GuFdST6

10. **Huff House Inn and Cabins:**

Huff House Inn and Cabins is a charming bed and breakfast that offers a warm and welcoming atmosphere with a focus on personalized service. The inn is located within walking distance of Jackson's town square, at 240 E Deloney Ave, Jackson, WY 83001, making it convenient for exploring the town's offerings. Huff House Inn and Cabins provide comfortable rooms and cozy cabins. The accommodations are thoughtfully decorated, creating a homey and inviting atmosphere. Guests can enjoy a delicious breakfast each morning and afternoon hors d'oeuvres, adding to the delightful experience. The inn offers a garden patio, a common living area with a fireplace, and access to the innkeepers' extensive local knowledge to enhance your stay. The number to call is +1 307-733-7141. To get to this inn on real time from Jackson Hole, click here for directions;
https://maps.app.goo.gl/ypSL9TG7J1qs4N4z9

Each of these inns in Jackson Hole has its own unique charm

and offerings, catering to a variety of traveler preferences and budgets. Depending on your priorities, whether it's location, amenities, or a serene atmosphere, you can choose the inn that best suits your needs and enjoy a delightful stay in this beautiful region.

2. Vacation Rentals:

If you prefer more privacy and a home-away-from-home feel, vacation rentals are a popular choice in Jackson Hole. You can find a number of options, including cabins, condos, and whole houses. Some popular sites for renting holiday rentals include Airbnb, Vrbo, and local property management firms. Vacation rentals are a terrific choice for families, groups of friends, or travelers who appreciate cooking their meals and having more room.

3. Guest Ranches:

Jackson Hole and the surrounding areas have a strong history of cattle ranching, and you can experience a taste of this tradition by staying at a guest ranch. These ranches provide a unique combination of luxury lodgings, horseback riding, and outdoor activities. Some well-known guest ranches in the region include:

- **Gros Ventre River Ranch**: Located east of the Teton Range, this ranch offers a gorgeous environment and activities including horseback riding, fly fishing, and hiking. For more queries dial +1 307-733-4138.

From Jackson to this ranch, click here for realtime directions: https://maps.app.goo.gl/URaPQRj6KDizxQiC7

- **Triangle X Ranch**: Situated inside Grand Teton National Park, this historic ranch provides a rare opportunity to remain within the park boundaries. Activities include horseback riding, fishing and nature viewing. For additional queries dial +1 307-733-2183.
    Click here for realtime instructions from Jackson: https://maps.app.goo.gl/dKoeKwuqT6e45EQ68

4. National Park Lodges:

If you plan to tour Grand Teton National Park or adjacent Yellowstone National Park, consider lodging at one of the national park lodges. These lodges offer rooms inside the parks, providing convenient access to the natural treasures of the region. Some prominent choices include:

- **Jackson Lake Resort**: Located in Grand Teton National Park, this resort overlooks Jackson Lake and offers beautiful views of the Teton Range. It's a prime site for those who wish to be immersed in the park's magnificence. For additional queries dial +1 307-543-2811.
    For real time instructions from Jackson go here: https://maps.app.goo.gl/EbprKjcng1zh81g86

Signal Mountain Lodge

- **Signal Mountain Resort**: Situated on the banks of Jackson Lake, this resort provides numerous accommodations, from lakefront cabins to hotel rooms. It's an excellent location for exploring both Grand Teton and Yellowstone National Parks. For inquiries dial +1 307-543-2831. For directions to go to the Lodge from Jackson in real-time, click here: https://maps.app.goo.gl/Zjehu i8vPjsApAPZ6

5. Campgrounds:

Jackson Hole is a haven for outdoor enthusiasts, and there are several campgrounds in the vicinity for those who prefer a more rustic and immersive experience. parks range from modest sites for tent camping to RV-friendly parks with connections. Some popular campgrounds include:

- **Gros Ventre Campground**: Located within Grand Teton National Park, this campground offers proximity to the Snake River and excellent vistas. As at the time of writing this, it's temporarily closed. However you can contact the National Park to know more at +1 307-543-2811.

- **Jenny Lake Campground**: Situated in the center of Grand Teton National Park, this campground provides a tranquil setting near Jenny Lake and various hiking routes. This campground is likewise temporarily closed today. However, you can discover more about what's happening by dialing+1 307-543-3100

Colter Bay Campground

- **Colter Bay Campground**: Inside Grand Teton National Park, this campground is close to the shores of Jackson Lake, affording spectacular lake views.

- **Yellowstone Campgrounds**: If you want to visit Yellowstone, you'll find a range of campgrounds within the park. Some take reservations, while others are first-come, first-served.

The following additional lodging advice can also help you plan/make decisions with regards to where to stay.

- **Book in Advance**: Especially during high seasons, it's essential to book your accommodations well in advance to guarantee your favorite choice and to ensure availability.

- **Stay Flexible**: If your travel dates are flexible, you may be able to locate better rates or discounts during less busy seasons of the year.

- **Check Cancellation terms**: Be sure to study the cancellation terms of your chosen accommodations, especially in the case of unforeseen changes to your travel plans.

- **Pet-Friendly Options**: If you're traveling with pets, consider accommodations that are pet-friendly, as some motels have unique restrictions surrounding pets.

- **Transportation Considerations:** When selecting your accommodation, think about the accessibility to your favorite activities and the availability of transportation choices, especially if you won't have a rental car.

III

The Culture

11

Dining and Cuisine

J ackson Hole's culinary scene reflects the area's raw yet sophisticated nature, with a variety of eateries honoring the creative influences of a diverse populace as well as Western traditions.

A beautiful blend of Western traditions and international influences may be found in Jackson Hole's culinary scene. The dining options here also reflect the multicultural makeup of the region's visitors and people, even though the American West's culinary legacy is honored with robust steaks, bison, and game meats.

Jackson Hole has a number of steakhouses where you may savor tender beef cuts that are frequently produced nearby. With their succulent steaks grilled to perfection, these restaurants epitomize the traditional Western dining experience.

Game meats such as bison and elk are mainstays in Jackson Hole's culinary scene for visitors looking for a taste of the wild. These distinctive meats are used in many restaurant menus, which feature recipes that honor the local culture.

Some restaurants offer chuckwagon dinners, which are a fun way to sample authentic Old West cuisine, in addition to standard dining options. In a rustic, Western-style environment, guests can enjoy meals cooked over an open fire.

With sushi bars and seafood shops serving up fresh catch from all over the world, Jackson Hole boasts a diversified culinary scene. In this landlocked Western jewel, you may have sushi rolls, sashimi, and fresh oysters.

With Mexican cantinas, Italian trattorias, and other international dining options strewn around the valley, a multitude of international flavors are represented. The area is enhanced by the diverse range of cuisines offered by these eateries.

One aspect of Jackson Hole's culinary industry that sets it apart is its dedication to using fresh, locally produced ingredients. In order to ensure that patrons enjoy the best produce the area has to offer, many restaurants and cafes proudly adhere to the farm-to-table mentality.

Weekly during the summer, locals and tourists can buy handmade products, artisanal cheeses, and fresh food grown nearby at the Jackson Hole Farmers Market. These locally derived ingredients are used in many meals at restaurants.

There are several ranches and farms in the area that provide fine meats, veggies, and other products to restaurants. Diners are guaranteed the freshest and tastiest ingredients because to the direct relationship between suppliers and chefs.

Places to eat

Many famous restaurants can be found in Jackson Hole, and each one adds something special to the area's gastronomic character.

1. **Snake River Grill**: You'll find this eatery at 84 E Broadway Ave, Jackson, WY 83001, United States.This well-liked eatery is praised for its inventive American fare and for utilizing regional ingredients in its menu. Dishes like wild boar and fish are available for diners to enjoy.

Million Dollar Cowboy Bar

2. **Million Dollar Cowboy Restaurant**: Mentioned earlier in this book, it's located in Jackson Hole, this iconic restaurant serves some of the best beef cuts in the area. For those looking for a real Western dining experience, the restaurant is a must-visit because of its traditional décor and Western vibe.

3. **Persephone Bakery**: Also at Broadway Avenue, Persephone Bakery is well-known for its handcrafted bread, pastries, and morning fare. A variety of baked goods are available for guests to savor with coffee or a quick breakfast in the center of Jackson.

4. **The Blue Lion**: Game meats and shellfish are served in this cozy eatery that combines flavors from around the world and the West. An inviting and comfortable mood is created by the lovely ambience, which includes a blazing fireplace.

Jackson Hole's Brewery Scene

Jackson Hole's craft beer and spirits market has been booming, with a number of brewers and distilleries leaving their stamp on the local culinary scene. In a relaxed setting, these places provide an opportunity to sample handcrafted beers and spirits from the area.

1. **Jackson Hole Still Works:** This distillery uses grains and other local ingredients to make a variety of spirits, such as whiskey, vodka, and gin. In addition to tasting creative drinks in the tasting area, visitors can tour the distillery.

2. **Snake River Brewing**: This is the oldest brewery in Jackson

Hole and is well-known for its inventive brews. Enjoying the breathtaking views of the mountains from the brewery's patio is paired perfectly with their extensive selection of beers.

The dynamic environment and apres-ski culture that character-ize Jackson Hole's eating scene are just as important as the great food. Following an exciting day of exploring the slopes or trails, a lot of tourists and locals congregate in pubs and restaurants to unwind, swap tales, and enjoy the companionship that comes with outdoor activities.

Skiers and snowboarders get together for apres-ski get-togethers at various restaurants and pubs to relax, take in live music, and raise a glass to an exciting day of exploration. The social component of dining in Jackson Hole enhances the experience even more.

Live music acts frequently accompany Jackson Hole's dining scene, adding to the lively ambiance. There's a diverse range of music available in the area, whether it's a well-known performer or a local band playing folk music.

Local products, less food waste, and a decrease in single-use plastics are just a few of the eco-friendly methods that Jackson Hole restaurants frequently employ. This sustainability pledge is in line with the area's commitment to protecting its natural heritage.

Food Festivals

Jackson Hole hosts a number of food festivals to showcase its delicious cuisine. These events bring the community together to enjoy the distinctive tastes of the American West and beyond.

The annual Jackson Hole Food & Wine Festival is a celebration of exquisite wines and gourmet food. In Jackson Hole, renowned chefs, winemakers, and culinary specialists get together to provide cooking lessons, wine tastings, and special dining experiences. With a breathtaking mountain backdrop, participants may become fully immersed in the art of food and wine pairing.

Taste of the Tetons is another festival, which takes place in the center of Jackson, showcases regional eateries, brewers, and food vendors. Participants get to taste a variety of foods, including favorites from the West and other cuisines. It is a lively and enjoyable festival with live music and family-friendly activities.

Old Bill's Fun Run for Charities is an annual community event that includes a "silly" parade with floats made around various topics, generally with a food theme. It's not only a food festival, though. In addition to wacky, food-themed floats, live music, and entertainment, spectators can enjoy the participation of local companies and organizations.

During what's called the Jackson Hole Wine Auction occasion, wine connoisseurs come together to sample fine wines from all over the world. It's a unique blend of epicurean delights and generosity, with the auction component supporting local organizations.

In addition to showcasing Jackson Hole's culinary skills, these food events highlight the area's commitment to protecting its natural history and helping the neighborhood. It doesn't matter whether you're an epicurean explorer or simply s lover of food, these festivals provide a delicious taste of Jackson Hole's distinct culinary culture

12

The Art

J ackson Hole, Wyoming, is a destination where the raw and untamed beauty of the American West meets a bustling arts and entertainment scene. Surrounded by the magnificent scenery of the Teton Range, the Snake River, and the Bridger-Teton National Forest, Jackson Hole has not only kept its Western legacy but has also nurtured a lively community of artists, musicians, and cultural lovers.

The awe-inspiring natural splendor of Jackson Hole serves as a wellspring of inspiration for artists and creators. The towering peaks of the Teton Range, the pristine alpine lakes, and the rolling stretches of sagebrush give a limitless canvas for artistic expression. Whether through painting, photography, or other art forms, Jackson Hole's environment has been a muse for generations of artists who've come to capture its beauty.

The visual arts scene in Jackson Hole is active and diverse, with various galleries and institutions presenting a wide range of artistic styles and mediums. The town of Jackson itself, along with its neighboring neighbor, Wilson, is home to a plethora of art places.

Nestled in a hillside overlooking the National Elk Refuge, National Museum of animals Art is a testament to the deep link between art and the region's animals. It features a vast collection of wildlife-themed art, including works by prominent artists including Carl Rungius and Bob Kuhn.

Jackson Hole Art Association (JHAA): Founded in 1965, the Jackson Hole Art Association (JHAA) is also a significant focus for visual arts in the town. It offers art lessons, exhibitions, and events, promoting the work of local artists.

The Jackson Hole Gallery Association represents approximately 30 galleries in the region, each presenting a unique collection of art. The monthly Gallery Walks offer the opportunity to explore the latest exhibitions and meet artists.

Furthermore, the Center for the Arts, a diverse arts center provides a space for artists, performers, and the community to come together. It provides art exhibitions, performances, and activities that promote the creative energy of Jackson Hole.

Jackson Hole has a long legacy of Western art, with many local artists focusing on Western themes and landscapes. This genre is profoundly ingrained in the region's history, and artists continue to represent the spirit of the American West.

While Western art remains a vital part of the scene, Jackson Hole is also home to contemporary artists who add a fresh, modern viewpoint to their work, frequently influenced by the surrounding natural splendor.

Music and Performing Arts

Jackson Hole's cultural offerings extend beyond visual arts, with a rich tapestry of music and performing arts that reflects the many interests of the population.

Held annually in the midst of the summer, the Grand Teton Music Festival invites world-class performers to perform a variety of classical and contemporary music. The festival's magnificent background, set against the Teton Range, improves the experience.

Jackson Hole Center for the Arts is an institution that acts as a cultural hub, offering a vast range of programs, from classical music to contemporary dance and theater. It's a space that supports artistic expression and appreciation.

Various places in Jackson Hole, such as the Silver Dollar Bar at the Wort Hotel, provide a stage for local and visiting performers. You may enjoy live music spanning a wide spectrum of genres, from country to jazz.

The Jackson Hole community has a profound passion for dance and theater. Local organizations and visiting performers offer a spectrum of performances, enriching the cultural scene.

Cultural Festivals and Events

Throughout the year, Jackson Hole holds a number of cultural festivals and events that showcase the region's heritage and creative spirit.

Held each September, the Fall Arts Festival is a highlight of the year. It contains a wide assortment of events, including artist receptions, quick-draw competitions, and auctions, all of which highlight the region's art culture.

Over Memorial Day weekend, Jackson Hole pays homage to its Western past with the Old West Days celebration. Events include parades, rodeos, and reenactments that transport tourists to the past.

Throughout the year, Jackson Hole offers several music and arts events that provide platforms for local and visiting performers to showcase their talents. These events bring art lovers and cultural enthusiasts from near and far.

Jackson Hole's cultural scene is strongly connected with the Western legacy of the region. Many artists and performers draw inspiration from the history and traditions of the American West, highlighting the continuing spirit of the region's pioneers and Native American civilizations.

Artistic representations of Western themes, from cowboy life to the spectacular wildlife of the Rockies, are common in Jackson Hole's galleries and performances. This cultural connection to the past acts as a reminder of the region's history, a history strongly tied to the land and its natural beauty.

Education and community interaction are vital components of Jackson Hole's arts and culture. Local organizations and institutions regularly engage with the community, creating chances for both residents and visitors to participate and learn. For instance the JHAA provides a range of art classes and workshops for artists of all ages and ability levels, encouraging artistic development and appreciation.

The National Museum of Wildlife Art and the Jackson Hole Center for the Arts offer educational programs that help the community enhance its understanding of art and its link to the region's natural world. Jackson Hole's cultural organizations enjoy considerable support from the local population. The arts are a fundamental element of Jackson Hole's identity, and inhabitants take pride in encouraging artistic expression.

13

Shopping and Souvenirs

One of the first things that strike visitors to Jackson Hole is its real Western vibe. Strolling around the streets of Jackson, you'll find various businesses specializing in Western attire, delivering a sense of the region's ranching and cowboy culture. Here, visitors get the opportunity to don traditional Western clothes, from cowboy boots to wide-brimmed hats, while also discovering a selection of unusual products.

Jackson Hole is a haven for individuals in search of high-quality cowboy boots and Western attire. Stores like 'Cowboy Corner' offer a large assortment of boots, belts, and clothes that embody the rugged and sophisticated Western character.

Also, If you've ever desired to own a custom-fitted Western hat, Jackson Hole boasts a number of hat shops that can make that dream a reality. These expert craftsmen design hats that are both useful and attractive.

As we've seen before now Jackson Hole is home to a thriving art community that draws inspiration from the surrounding landscapes and cowboy culture. Visitors can explore several art galleries and stores that feature paintings, sculptures, and other art forms symbolizing the American West.

In a place with a rich history of rodeo activities, it's no wonder that you can buy an array of rodeo gear and equipment in local shops. Whether you're a seasoned rider or just a fan of the rodeo, you'll find all you need here.

The region's link to Native American culture is evident in the range of establishments that offer Native American crafts and art. Jewelry, pottery, and textiles are among the many gifts that honor indigenous artistry.

For those interested in unusual findings and vintage treasures, Jackson Hole has various antique and vintage shops where you can uncover objects that reflect the history of the area.

Local Boutiques and Unique Souvenirs

Beyond Western attire and cowboy gear, Jackson Hole provides an array of local boutiques and businesses that give a wide selection of unique souvenirs, apparel, and home decor. These boutiques generally offer locally crafted things with a dash of Western flair.

If you're interested in home decor, many shops specialize in home decor and furnishings that evoke the spirit of Jackson

85

Hole and the Wild West. From rustic furniture to distinctive home accessories, you'll find products that lend a touch of the West to your house.

Jackson Hole is also home to a flourishing community of artisans and craftsmen who create unique, handcrafted goods. Local markets and boutiques regularly display their works, including pottery, woodworking, and more.

The region is famed for its magnificent gemstones, including Jackson Hole jade and opal. You can find jewelry businesses that offer a selection of gemstone pieces, often created by local artisans.

Markets and Fairs

Visitors to Jackson Hole have the opportunity to immerse themselves in the local culture by attending various markets, fairs, and festivals. These events are often rich in tradition and provide a unique shopping experience.

1. Jackson Hole Farmers Market: A lively weekly event during the summer months, the Jackson Hole Farmers Market is where locals and visitors can find fresh produce, artisanal foods, and handmade goods from the region.

2. Art and Craft Fairs: Throughout the year, Jackson Hole hosts various art and craft fairs, where local artisans showcase their creations. These fairs are an ideal place to discover unique, handcrafted items and meet the people who make them.

3. Rodeo Markets: In conjunction with the rodeo events in Jackson Hole, rodeo markets often feature a variety of Western-themed merchandise, from cowboy gear to local crafts.

IV

National Parks and Scenic Areas

We have mentioned a number of these parks and scenic areas in previous chapters. Here we'll be learning about them in detail. Let's go!

14

Grand Teton National Park

G rand Teton National Park is a spectacular natural wonder that invites travelers with its majestic mountain
peaks, pristine alpine lakes, and a rich tapestry of
wildlife. This spectacular national park, generally referred to
simply as "the Tetons," is a paradise for outdoor enthusiasts,
hikers, photographers, and nature lovers.

At the center of Grand Teton National Park rises the Teton Range, a majestic and awe-inspiring mountain range that has enthralled tourists for decades. The park receives its name from the Grand Teton, the largest peak in the range, which rises to an elevation of 13,770 feet (4,197 meters). This prominent peak, along with its adjacent summits, offers a stunning background that graces numerous postcards, pictures, and paintings.

The Teton Range is defined by its jagged, granite spires, soaring summits, and spectacular glacier valleys. These peaks, frequently buried in snow, serve as a magnificent canvas for both sunrise and sunset, creating a warm alpenglow over the landscape that's a sight to behold.

Grand Teton National Park is home to a broad range of ecosystems, which flourish in the varying elevations and climatic circumstances. The park ranges from the low-lying valley floors to the towering peaks of the Teton Range. These distinct ecosystems provide home for a diverse range of species.

The park is a sanctuary for an abundance of species. Elk, moose, bison, mule deer, and pronghorn can be often sighted in the valley. Grizzly bears, black bears, wolves, and coyotes frequent the region, affording a chance for wildlife enthusiasts to witness these spectacular species.

Grand Teton National Park is also a haven for birdwatchers. The park hosts several species of raptors, ducks, and songbirds. It's a crucial migratory stopover for many bird species, offering superb bird watching possibilities throughout the year.

As you rise into the alpine regions of the Teton Range, you'll see alpine meadows, pristine glacier lakes, and hardy plants suited to the severe high-altitude environment.

The park is traversed by the Snake River, which supports riparian ecosystems abounding with birdlife, beavers, and other aquatic animals.

Recreational Opportunities

Grand Teton National Park is a playground for outdoor enthusiasts, offering a wide range of recreational possibilities that allow visitors to immerse themselves in the natural splendor.

1. **Hiking**: The park has a network of hiking paths appropriate for all skill levels. Whether you're taking a leisurely stroll around Jenny Lake or embarking on a hard backcountry excursion,

hiking in the Tetons gives an intimate connection with the breathtaking surroundings.

2. **Camping:** Grand Teton National Park includes various campgrounds that accommodate both tent and RV campers. Camping amidst the park's unspoiled environment provides for an authentic experience under the starlit skies.

3. **Scenic Drives:** The park's scenic byways, such as the Teton Park Road, offer stunning vistas of the Teton Range and access to historic structures like the Chapel of the Transfiguration and the Snake River Overlook, made famous by Ansel Adams' photography.

4. **Boating and Rafting:** Jenny Lake and Jackson Lake are perfect for boating, kayaking, and canoeing. The Snake River offers opportunity for gorgeous float rides and thrilling whitewater rafting.

5. **Fishing:** Anglers can cast their hooks into the Snake River and its tributaries, where they may catch a variety of trout species, including cutthroat and brown trout.

6. **Skiing and Winter Recreation**: In the winter months, Grand Teton National Park transforms into a winter paradise. Skiing, snowshoeing, and snowmobiling are popular activities. The park's beautiful snowy landscapes are a dream for winter sports aficionados.

7. **Guided Tours**: The park offers guided tours, including wildlife safaris, photographic trips, and ranger-led programs

that provide deeper insights into the area's natural and cultural heritage.

The preservation of Grand Teton National Park is a monument to the determination of individuals who saw the need to conserve this spectacular area. The park's story is one of conservation, including the successful efforts of John D. Rockefeller Jr., who played a crucial role in guaranteeing the protection of the Teton Range and its surrounding valleys.

The formation of the park was a crucial point in the history of American conservation, and it shows the nation's dedication to preserving its natural heritage for future generations.

15

Yellowstone National Park

Lower Falls in Yellowstone Park

Yellowstone National Park, situated largely in the U.S. state of Wyoming but extending into Montana and Idaho, is a natural wonderland that has captured the minds of visitors for well over a century. Established as the world's first national park in 1872, Yellowstone is recognized for its geothermal features, diversified ecosystems, and rich wildlife. This enthralling park is a monument to the strength and beauty of the natural world, providing tourists a journey through geysers, hot springs, forests, and expansive vistas.

One of the most distinctive elements of Yellowstone is its geothermal wonders. The park is home to almost half of the world's geysers, including the world-famous Old Faithful, which erupts frequently with clockwork accuracy. Visitors from around the globe gather to witness spectacular eruptions that send columns of scalding water and steam high into the air.

Grand Prismatic Spring

Yellowstone's geothermal environment is littered with colorful hot springs, such as the Grand Prismatic Spring, which exhibits bright hues ranging from deep blue to blazing orange. These natural wonders are the result of superheated water packed with minerals that rise from the Earth's depths, creating unique and ever-changing geological formations.

Mud pots, fumaroles, and terraces add to the park's geothermal extravaganza. The geothermal zones are not only intriguing but also serve as reminders of the volatile nature of the Earth's crust, where magma lurks just beneath the surface.

Yellowstone National Park is home to an assortment of varied ecosystems that provide habitats for a wide range of wildlife. The park's forests, meadows, rivers, and lakes offer shelter and sustenance to a varied tapestry of species.

Yellowstone is recognized for its iconic fauna, including bison, elk, moose, grizzly bears, black bears, and wolves. The park is a critical refuge for species that have faced danger of extinction, including the gray wolf. The successful reintroduction of wolves to the park in the 1990s marked a key milestone in wildlife conservation.

Also, the park is a birder's delight. With over 300 kinds of birds, including bald eagles, ospreys, and sandhill cranes, it offers superb birdwatching opportunities.

The park's rivers and lakes are filled with numerous trout species, making it a favored destination for anglers.

The park actively invests in ecosystem restoration initiatives to protect the natural balance of the region. Initiatives include the management of non-native species and the restoration of native flora and animals.

Recreational Opportunities

Yellowstone National Park has a huge range of recreational options, catering to a broad spectrum of interests and skills.

1. **Hiking:** The park features a wide network of hiking trails, allowing chances for short day treks, backcountry backpacking, and everything in between. The trails lead to magnificent landscapes, geothermal features, and hidden waterfalls.

2. **Camping:** Yellowstone includes various campgrounds, from rustic sites to RV-friendly settings. Camping in the park allows guests to interact with nature and enjoy the splendor of the night sky.

3. **Fauna Watching**: The park's plentiful fauna gives a fantastic opportunity for wildlife watchers and photographers. Guided wildlife trips can enhance the experience, improving the chances of viewing elusive animals.

4. **Scenic Drives**: The park's roadways snake across its beautiful landscapes, allowing opportunity to witness geological wonders, wildlife, and renowned sights such as Yellowstone Lake.

5. **Fishing**: Visitors can enjoy fishing in the park's rivers,

streams, and lakes. A fishing license is necessary, and controls are in place to safeguard native fish populations.

6. **Winter Recreation**: While the summer months draw the majority of visitors, Yellowstone is equally enthralling in winter. Snowshoeing, cross-country skiing, snowmobiling, and wildlife watching are popular winter activities.

7. **Boating and Rafting:** Yellowstone Lake and the park's rivers are great for boating, kayaking, and rafting. Guided float tours along the Yellowstone River provide a unique perspective of the park's beauty.

Yellowstone's history is connected with the growth of the United States westward, and it possesses cultural and historical value. Native American tribes have long had connections to the country, and early explorers like John Colter and fur trappers went into the region.

The park's formation as the first national park in the world was a watershed moment in the conservation movement. The preservation of Yellowstone set a precedent for the protection of natural wonders, and it served as a model for the development of national parks worldwide.

While Yellowstone is famous for its natural beauty and conservation initiatives, it is not immune to difficulties. Climate change, invasive species, and human impact are issues of concern. Rising temperatures, changing migration patterns, and the growth of non-native plants and animals are concerns that the park must address in its efforts to conserve the environment.

16

Bridger-Teton National Forest

Bridger-Teton National Forest, located in western Wyoming, is a huge and unspoiled wilderness that stands as one of the jewels of the U.S. Forest Service system. Encompassing about 3.4 million acres, it is one of the largest national forests in the United States. Bridger-Teton is famous for its stunning scenery, including the towering Wind River Range, lush woods, plentiful wildlife, and countless recreational options. This huge forest is a paradise for outdoor enthusiasts, wildlife lovers, and those seeking a deep connection with the natural world.

Bridger-Teton National Forest's geography is immensely diversified, ranging from lowland sagebrush and meadows to rocky alpine peaks and deep gorges. The forest is home to some of the most prominent mountain ranges in the Rocky Mountains, including the Wind River Range, the Teton Range, the Gros Ventre Range, and the Wyoming Range. The towering peaks of the Wind River Range include Gannett Peak, Wyoming's highest point at 13,809 feet (4,209 meters).

The forest is crisscrossed by innumerable rivers and streams, including the Green River and the Snake River. The region's waterways not only sustain a variety of aquatic life but also offer good chances for fishing and water-based recreation.

Bridger-Teton National Forest provides a shelter for a vast assortment of species. The forest's environments support countless species, from huge mammals to birds, fish, and tiny invertebrates.

The forest is home to iconic animals such as moose, elk, mule deer, and pronghorn. Grizzly bears, black bears, mountain lions, and wolves are also present within its limits. The forest plays a significant role in the protection and management of these species.

Bird aficionados will find the forest a sanctuary for birdwatching. A great variety of raptors, songbirds, and ducks can be viewed throughout the area.

Bridger-Teton also offers outstanding chances for fishermen. Its streams and lakes are rich with several trout species, including cutthroat, rainbow, and brown trout.

Recreational Opportunities

Bridger-Teton National Forest provides a comprehensive choice of recreational possibilities for tourists, ensuring that everyone can find an activity to enjoy in this immense wilderness.

1. **Hiking:** The forest offers a multitude of hiking trails appropriate for all skill levels. Trails lead to alpine lakes, mountain peaks, and pure wilderness areas. Notable paths include the Bridger Wilderness paths and the Wind River Range routes.

2. **Camping:** Campers can select from a range of campgrounds, some equipped with contemporary conveniences, while others provide a more basic camping experience. Camping in the forest allows guests to experience the natural beauty and solitude of the area.

3. **Horseback Riding**: Equestrians can explore the forest's pathways and meadows on horseback. Guided horseback riding experiences are also provided for individuals new to horse riding.

4. **Mountain Biking:** The forest contains mountain biking tracks that vary in difficulty, from easy rides along forest roads to hard

singletrack routes.

5. **Hunting:** Bridger-Teton National Forest is open to hunting during defined seasons, giving possibilities for those interested in big game and small game hunting.

6. **Boating and Rafting:** The forest's rivers and lakes are great for boating, kayaking, and rafting. Guided float tours down the Snake River provide a unique way to explore the forest's beauty.

7. **Scenic Drives**: Several Scenic byways and forest roads wind through the forest, allowing opportunity to explore its splendor from the comfort of a vehicle.

8. **Winter Recreation**: During the winter months, Bridger-Teton transforms into a winter playground. Snowmobiling, cross-country skiing, snowshoeing, and ice fishing are popular winter activities.

9. **Fauna Viewing**: Observing the forest's fauna is a popular pastime. With adequate protection and respect for the animals, visitors can view the area's amazing fauna.

10. **Backpacking and Mountaineering**: The forest is a refuge for backpackers and mountaineers, with huge backcountry areas, high alpine peaks, and pristine lakes ready to be explored.

Bridger-Teton National Forest offers cultural and historical value for the region. Native American groups, notably the Shoshone and Crow, have long lasting relationships to the land. Early European explorers and fur trappers, like as Jim Bridger and Kit Carson, traveled into the area, leaving behind a historical heritage that is still recognized.

The forest also plays a role in continuing archaeological and historical studies, offering light on the region's pre-European history and its significance for indigenous peoples.

17

National Elk Refuge

Somewhere in the heart of Jackson Hole, Wyoming, the National Elk Refuge stands as a tribute to the conservation of North America's natural heritage. Spanning over 24,700 acres of unspoiled wilderness, the refuge is recognized for its principal occupants, the North American elk, but it also provides protection for a varied range of other species. Established to protect and sustain elk herds throughout the harsh winters, the refuge has evolved into a symbol of animal conservation, affording visitors the opportunity to connect with nature and experience the extraordinary adaptations that species make to survive in the brutal winter settings.

The National Elk Refuge was formed in 1912 with a clear mission: to provide a winter habitat for the Jackson Elk Herd, one of the largest elk herds in North America. These gorgeous beasts had been brutally hunted and driven from their typical winter grounds, putting their survival at jeopardy.In the early years, the refuge encountered tremendous difficulty in supplying appropriate food for the elk during the winter. To solve this issue, the refuge developed a supplemental feeding program, which continues to this day. This initiative involves the provision of hay to elk during the winter months, ensuring they have sufficient sustenance to withstand the hard conditions.

The refuge's aim has subsequently extended to embrace the conservation of a wide variety of animals, including bison, mule deer, pronghorn, trumpeter swans, and a plethora of other birds. In addition to providing habitat for these species, the refuge also encourages education, research, and wildlife management to protect the long-term health of its populations.

Mountain Elk

The National Elk Refuge is located at the southern fringe of the Greater Yellowstone Ecosystem, one of the last surviving practically complete temperate ecosystems on Earth. This unique location makes it a key component of the ecology and the natural world. The refuge's diverse habitats, including marshes, grasslands, and shrublands, provide excellent resources for a diversity of wildlife.

1. **Elk**: The refuge serves as a critical winter range for elk, where they find the essential food and shelter to survive. The supplementary feeding program helps support elk numbers through the difficult winter months.

2. **Bison**: Bison are another notable species in the sanctuary. As one of the few areas where wild bison are maintained in their original habitat, the refuge provides a key ecosystem for these iconic creatures.

3. **Birds**: The refuge's wetlands attract a diverse diversity of bird species, including trumpeter swans, bald eagles, and a myriad of waterfowl. It's a significant stopover location for migratory birds.

4. **Mule Deer and Pronghorn**: Mule deer and pronghorn are also part of the refuge's complex environment. They seek refuge and sustenance within the protected area throughout the winter months.

Recreational Opportunities and Education

The National Elk Refuge offers visitors a rare opportunity to engage with wildlife and the conservation activities that preserve it. The refuge's visitor center includes a plethora of information on the area's history, animals, and active conservation programs.

One of the most renowned ways to explore the refuge is with a guided sled ride. These trips allow tourists to get up close and personal with the elk herds while watching the meticulous management of their winter habitat.

Wildlife enthusiasts can explore the refuge in search of bison, mule deer, pronghorn, and a variety of bird species. The refuge's diversified ecosystems offer numerous chances for birdwatching.

The refuge offers educational programs that teach visitors about wildlife conservation and the necessity of protecting natural habitats.

For photographers, the refuge provides a unique and stunning backdrop for capturing the splendor of wildlife in a pristine, natural setting.

While the National Elk Refuge has made considerable progress in maintaining wildlife, it faces continuous problems. Climate change, invasive species, and disease control are major challenges that must be addressed. Rising temperatures and shifting precipitation patterns can alter the timing of elk migrations and the availability of food.

Invasive species like cheatgrass damage the native plant communities of the refuge, which in turn impacts the wildlife that depend on these plants for food. Additionally, disease control is an issue, as animal populations are prone to diseases like chronic wasting disease and brucellosis.

18

Teton Pass Scenic Byway

The Teton Pass Scenic Byway winds through some of the most stunning scenery in the country and is situated close to Jackson Hole, Wyoming, in the heart of the Rocky Mountains. Travelers can enjoy broad valley views, verdant forests, and panoramic views of the Teton Range as they travel 37 miles across Teton Pass. The byway is a destination in and of itself, renowned for its natural splendor, outdoor recreational options, and the sense of wonder it evokes in everyone who ventures along its serpentine course. It serves as a gateway to the unspoiled wilderness of the Grand Teton and Bridger-Teton National Forests.

The Teton Pass Scenic Byway starts in Victor, Idaho, and winds its way through scenic valleys, past lakes in the alpine region, and finally crosses into Wyoming's western region. The Teton Range is traversed by the byway, opening doors to some of the area's most breathtaking natural splendor.

The Big Hole Mountains' peaks provide a breathtaking backdrop as visitors follow Idaho State Highway 33 for the first section of the byway. A preview of the spectacular scenery to come is provided by the road's winding eastward course. Summertime wildflower meadows along the route provide vivid bursts of color to the surroundings.

The experience of climbing Teton Pass is quite amazing. Many switchbacks on the highway are designed to take drivers to an elevation of 8,431 feet (2,570 meters). The scenery gets more spectacular as you ascend, with broad vistas of the breathtaking Teton Range to the east and the Snake River Range to the west.

A pull-off location at the top of Teton Pass offers the ideal spot to stop and admire the majesty of the Tetons. Interpretive signs at the viewpoint provide information about the area's geological past, as well as the flora and fauna that call this high-altitude habitat home. The wildflowers are at their peak in the summer, and in the winter, this is a well-liked place to begin backcountry skiing and snowmobiling excursions.

The byway offers stunning vistas of the Teton Range and the Snake River Valley as it descends into Wilson, Wyoming, following an exciting climb up Teton Pass. You'll pass through thick forests, undulating hills, and the Snake River flowing as you descend.

Because it offers a another viewpoint of the steep landscape, the descent is just as interesting as the ascent. The beautiful valley below is dramatically contrasted with the rugged peaks of the Tetons, which loom in the distance.

Recreational Opportunities

The Teton Pass Scenic Byway is a gateway to an extensive range of outdoor recreational options, not merely a road through breathtaking vistas. The byway has plenty to offer everyone, whether they are mountain bikers, hikers, skiers, or just lovers of the great outdoors.

1. **Hiking:** A system of hiking paths that connects to the byway leads to alpine lakes, picturesque views, and unspoiled nature. In the area, hikes to Phillips Pass, Bradley Lake, and Taggart Lake are well-liked.

2. **Mountain Biking**: For those who enjoy mountain biking, this place is a paradise. The paths surrounding Teton Pass are renowned for their breathtaking scenery and difficult terrain.

3. Skiing and Snowmobiling: The byway transforms into a winter paradise in the wintertime. Snowmobiling and backcountry skiing are popular in the Teton Pass region. Winter sports enthusiasts looking for untracked powder travel to this location.

4. Observing Wildlife: A wide range of wildlife can be seen in the Snake River Valley, including moose, elk, deer, and several bird species.

5. Cultural Exploration: Wilson, a nearby town, provides opportunities to visit local art galleries, eat at quaint restaurants, and discover the history of the area.

The Teton Pass Scenic Byway passes through the center of the Greater Yellowstone Ecosystem, which is well-known for its unspoiled scenery and rich wildlife. One of the planet's few almost-intact temperate habitats is this one.

In order to maintain this area as a wildlife sanctuary and a popular travel destination for outdoor enthusiasts, conservation efforts are made to save the ecosystem and biodiversity of the area. To protect this natural treasure, actions including conserving wildlife corridors, controlling invasive species, and encouraging appropriate outdoor enjoyment are essential.

V

Day Trips and Excursions

19

Snake River Float Trips

Jackson Hole is a gateway to magnificent natural beauty, and there's no better way to enjoy this than to get involved in a Snake River Float Trips. This excursion takes you along the meandering Snake River, where you'll immerse yourself in the calm terrain, witness wildlife, and receive a fresh perspective on the diverse ecosystems of the region.

Snake River

Your day begins with an early morning trip from Jackson Hole. The drive to Snake River Float Trips takes just over 20 minutes, providing the perfect chance to appreciate the scenic grandeur of Jackson Hole on your way to the river. The Snake River, with its gentle meanders and abundant riparian habitats, offers a quiet and picturesque setting for a day of leisure and discovery.

Upon arrival at Snake River Float Trips, you'll be greeted by professional guides who will be your companions for the day. They are not only competent river pilots but also knowledgeable naturalists who can give insights into the region's flora and fauna.

Before you leave on your float trip, you'll have the opportunity to pick between scenic and whitewater float experiences, each giving a distinct experience.

Scenic floats are great for people seeking a leisurely, serene experience. These floats take you around the smooth portions of the Snake River, enabling you to absorb the grandeur of the surrounding environment, watch wildlife, and take in the serene mood.

For those who seek a bit more excitement, whitewater float experiences are available. These adventures offer an exciting journey through the river's rapids, blending the calm of the natural environment with moments of exhilaration.

Wildlife Viewing: A Pristine Habitat

The Snake River and its neighboring riparian areas are alive with animals. From the boat, you'll have fantastic opportunities to view diverse species that make this region home. Keep your eyes peeled for:

Bald Eagles: The Snake River is home to a healthy population of bald eagles, and you may spot these majestic birds perched in trees along the riverbanks or soaring overhead.

Moose: The riverbanks and nearby wetlands provide ideal habitat for moose. It's common to see these massive creatures wading through the water or grazing on aquatic vegetation.

Elk and Deer: Elk and mule deer are often seen along the river's edge, especially during the early morning or evening hours. Their presence adds a touch of wilderness to your float experience.

Beaver Dams and Lodges: The Snake River is dotted with beaver dams and lodges, and you may observe these industrious creatures at work or hear the gentle slap of their tails against the water.

River Otters: River otters are playful inhabitants of the Snake River, and it's a delight to watch them swim and frolic in the water.

Birdlife: The riparian habitat along the river is a haven for a variety of bird species. You'll have the opportunity to spot waterfowl, songbirds, and possibly a great blue heron or osprey.

As you float along the river, you'll be surrounded by the geological wonders of the region. The Snake River has played a pivotal role in carving the valley and shaping the landscape over thousands of years. Your guides can offer explanations about the geological forces that have shaped this environment, adding depth to your understanding of the natural world.

Your float trip will include a picnic lunch along the riverbanks. Enjoy a leisurely meal amidst the tranquility of the Snake River. You'll have the chance to relax, savor a delicious picnic spread, and reflect on the scenic beauty and wildlife encounters of your journey.

The Snake River holds historical significance for Native American tribes in the region, particularly the Shoshone and Bannock. Your guides can share insights into the cultural and historical importance of the river to these tribes, as well as their traditional uses of the waterway.

Depending on your preference, you can choose between guided rafting trips or more independent canoeing adventures. Both options provide a chance to get up close and personal with the river.

The Snake River is not just a playground for outdoor enthusiasts but also a place for peaceful reflection. As you float along, you'll have moments of solitude and tranquility. It's a time to connect with the natural world, leave behind the noise of everyday life, and appreciate the serenity of the river.

The Snake River banks are adorned with wildflowers during the spring and early summer. Depending on the season of your visit, you may witness a colorful display of lupine, Indian paintbrush, and other native wildflowers.

As the late afternoon sets in, you'll conclude your Snake River Float Trip and head back to Jackson Hole. The drive back provides a final opportunity to savor the scenic beauty of the region. The sunlight casts a warm, golden hue over the valley, enhancing the grandeur of the landscape.

Your day trip from Jackson Hole to Snake River Float Trips concludes in the vibrant town of Jackson Hole. Consider stopping for dinner at one of the town's restaurants, where you can share your experiences and enjoy local cuisine.

20

Grand Targhee Resort

P erched on the western slope of the renowned Teton Mountains, Grand Targhee Resort is a hidden gem in the heart of Wyoming. It's a place where outdoor enthusiasts and nature lovers come to enjoy the majesty of the American West, from the magnificent scenery to the exhilarating activities.

Grand Targhee Resort located amidst the Caribou-Targhee National Forest, a natural wilderness that provides some of the most spectacular mountain landscapes in the country. The resort is situated on the western slope of the Teton Range, affording panoramic views of the Grand Teton, the largest peak in the range, and the surrounding peaks. This setting makes it a year-round destination for outdoor sports and natural beauty.

Winter is when Grand Targhee Resort fully comes alive. With an average yearly snowfall of nearly 500 inches, this is a powder paradise for skiers and snowboarders. The resort includes approximately 2,500 acres of skiable terrain, including groomed lines, glades, and powder bowls. The light, fluffy snow that blankets the slopes has earned Grand Targhee a reputation as one of the top locations for powder seekers.

One of the trademarks of Grand Targhee Resort is its family-friendly atmosphere. The resort's laid-back feel and large selection of beginner and intermediate terrain make it a pleasant spot for families with skiers and snowboarders of all ages. It's a great venue for introducing children to the enjoyment of winter sports.

For those who prefer a calmer, more contemplative winter experience, Grand Targhee Resort offers nearly 15 kilometers of groomed cross-country ski slopes, as well as backcountry paths for more daring explorers. Snowshoers will also find a winter wonderland to uncover on the routes that meander through pristine woodlands and wide meadows.

Grand Targhee Ski Resort

When the snow melts and summer arrives, Grand Targhee Resort transforms into a beautiful mountain wonderland. The rolling hills become a sea of wildflowers, and the resort becomes a hub for hiking, mountain biking, and music festivals.

The resort's wide network of mountain bike tracks gives opportunities for cyclists of all ability levels. From easy, family-friendly rides to difficult downhill slopes, there's a trail for everyone. The stunning views of the Tetons are a gift for those who hit the trails on two wheels.

Grand Targhee Resort is the gateway to a hiking nirvana. The several paths that start from the resort range from short, instructive nature walks to strenuous, full-day hikes that lead to breathtaking vistas and alpine lakes.

Summer is also when the resort comes alive with music. The Grand Targhee Bluegrass Festival, Targhee Fest, and other events bring renowned performers to the mountain for an unparalleled outdoor musical experience.

The fascination of Grand Targhee Resort extends far beyond its recreational activities. The mountain vistas, wildflower-covered meadows, and untouched wildness form a backdrop that's both intriguing and tranquil. It's a place to connect with the natural world, whether you're hiking through the forest, riding on the trails, or simply soaking in the views from the resort's numerous vantage points.

As a part of the pristine Caribou-Targhee National Forest, Grand Targhee Resort lays a major emphasis on conservation and sustainability. The resort makes steps to reduce its environmental impact, conserve the natural surrounds, and teach visitors about the need of conservation. This dedication to stewardship guarantees that the natural beauty and outdoor recreation opportunities remain for future generations to enjoy.

Grand Targhee Resort isn't just a resort; it's a community of outdoor enthusiasts who share a love for the mountains and a passion for adventure. The inviting atmosphere at the resort generates a sense of kinship among tourists. It's not uncommon to pick up talks with fellow travelers on the chairlift or at the base lodge.

The resort is not only a venue for outdoor adventures but also a cultural nexus in the region. In addition to the summer music festivals, Grand Targhee hosts a range of events throughout the year. From art exhibitions to workshops and educational activities, these events provide visitors an opportunity to connect with the local culture and arts.

Grand Targhee Resort is also home to a rich assortment of fauna. While hiking, riding, or skiing in the area, it's typical to encounter elk, moose, deer, and a variety of bird species. The devotion to conservation at the resort adds to the increasing animal population in the region.

Grand Targhee Resort is a year-round resort for individuals who appreciate the grandeur of the Tetons. Whether it's a winter trip to ski in the powder, a summer escape to hike and enjoy live music, or a fall adventure to observe the changing leaves, the resort offers a wide choice of activities and experiences to appeal to every season.

21

The Wind River Range

J ackson Hole is, as we have stated over and over again, famed for its gorgeous landscapes and outdoor adventures, but for those seeking a wilderness vacation that's off the beaten road, a day drive to the Wind River Range in Dubois provides a voyage into pristine grandeur.

Your day begins early as you head off from Jackson Hole. The travel to Dubois takes roughly two to three hours, but it's a journey filled with breathtaking beauty. You'll head east, leaving behind the bustling tourist town of Jackson Hole and into the wide expanse of the Wyoming wilderness. The drive itself is a vital element of the day excursion, as you pass through varied scenery, from open plains to forested mountain roads.

While en route, consider making a few picturesque stops to admire the beauty of the region:

About 20 miles east of Jackson, you'll reach Togwotee Pass. Stop at one of the many pull-offs to appreciate the panoramic beauty of the Teton Range. In the summer, this location offers fantastic opportunity for wildflower watching.

Continue down Highway 26 and you'll pass past Brooks Lake. The view of the lake, encircled by the Absaroka Mountains, is spectacular. If time allows, try stopping here for a short hike or simply to appreciate the calm alpine landscape.

By mid-morning, you'll arrive at Dubois, a lovely hamlet tucked at the base of the Wind River Range. Begin your journey by relaxing in for a wonderful lunch at one of the local eateries. Here, you may enjoy the flavors of Wyoming with dishes that generally feature fresh, locally produced ingredients.

After your hearty lunch, make your way to the Dubois Museum. This cultural hub presents the tale of the area's history, from the days of early explorers and trappers to the growth of the town. The museum offers an array of antiques, images, and displays that provide a fascinating peek into the region's legacy.

With historical context in mind, you're now ready to embark on your wilderness expedition. The Fitzpatrick Wilderness, part of the Shoshone National Forest, offers a plethora of hiking options. Many trailheads are accessible from the Dubois area, and the terrain ranges from moderate treks to strenuous backpacking trips.

Depending on your interests and the time available, you can choose a trailhead that meets your group's ability. Some popular trailheads are Whiskey Mountain, Whiskey Creek, and Union Pass. Each offers a unique hiking experience, from meandering through wildflower meadows to rising into high alpine peaks.

Keep a keen eye out for animals, since the Fitzpatrick Wilderness is home to varied species, including mule deer, moose, elk, and a variety of bird species. You may observe a moose grazing beside a stream or hear the mournful call of a loon on one of the alpine lakes.

As you hike, you'll be surrounded by the rugged splendor of the Wind River Range. The Rocky Mountains rise before you, and exquisite alpine lakes reflect the clear blue Wyoming sky. The scenery is a photographer's paradise, so be sure to capture the breathtaking sights throughout the trail.

The Fitzpatrick Wilderness offers a range of activities to enjoy during your day adventure.

Continue your journey, exploring deeper into the forest, and perhaps placing your sights on a certain destination or spectacular viewpoint. The immensity of the Wind River Range guarantees that you have numerous options to select from.

If you're a fishing enthusiast, many of the alpine lakes in the vicinity give the opportunity to cast your line. These lakes are noted for their crystal-clear waters and abundance of trout, making them great for fly fishing.

Find a calm area to rest and soak in the tranquility of the environment. You can simply enjoy the sound of nature, meditate beside a mountain stream, or read a book while appreciating the quiet of the natural world.

As the early evening creeps in, it's time to drive back to Jackson Hole. The return ride provides yet another opportunity to view the gorgeous landscapes. The trip in the golden hour of late afternoon or early evening is particularly wonderful, as the sun creates a warm, mellow glow over the mountains and valleys.

On your drive back to Jackson Hole, consider stopping for dinner at one of the restaurants in Dubois. It's an opportunity to sample local cuisine once more and to reflect on the day's wilderness journey.

Your day journey from Jackson Hole to the Wind River Range in Dubois has come to an end as you return to the colorful town of Jackson Hole. With a sense of fulfillment and respect for the natural beauty of the Wind River Range, you may look forward to a pleasant night's rest in the comfort of your Jackson Hole lodging.

22

Idaho Falls

L ocated just a few of hours away, Idaho Falls is a lovely city along the Snake River, recognized for its scenic beauty, cultural attractions, and rich history.

Your day begins early as you depart from Jackson Hole for Idaho Falls. The travel to Idaho Falls takes around two to three hours, depending on your selected route. This excursion provides a terrific opportunity to soak in the spectacular vistas that Wyoming has to offer.

There are two primary routes to reach Idaho Falls from Jackson Hole, each offering its own picturesque attractions:

Teton Pass Route: This route takes you through Teton Pass, which offers amazing panoramic views of the Teton Range. You'll drop into the Teton Valley and pass through picturesque communities like Victor and Driggs.

Swan Valley Route: The Swan Valley route follows the Snake River, affording magnificent views of the river and neighboring farms. It's noted for its serene beauty and good animal viewing chances.

Upon arriving in Idaho Falls, you'll be met with the tranquil and gorgeous Snake River. The city is recognized for its riverside parks, spectacular waterfalls, and an inviting ambiance that promotes exploration.

Snake River Greenbelt: The Snake River Greenbelt is a 5-mile-long pathway that meanders along the river, offering picturesque views, picnic places, and a chance to stretch your legs. It's a fantastic setting for a leisurely morning stroll.

137

Spend some time visiting the city's waterfront, where you can enjoy the splendor of the Snake River and take in views of the famed Idaho Falls. This natural wonder is a series of cascading waterfalls that were originally developed for hydroelectric power and have now become a beloved feature of the city.

Your morning trip can continue with a visit to the Museum of Idaho, a cultural hub in the city that provides a view into the region's history, culture, and traditions.

The museum offers a range of exhibits, including those on the Lewis and Clark Expedition, the Civil War, and the history of the city and the surrounding region. Each exhibit offers a chance to dive into different parts of the past.

The museum is not merely a venue for historical objects but also an educational resource. It provides insights about the people, events, and cultures that have shaped the area.

After your tour to the museum, head to downtown Idaho Falls for lunch at one of the local eateries. The city's downtown is lovely, featuring a mix of restaurants and stores that represent the flavor of the community.

Savor local flavors with recipes that often combine fresh, locally produced ingredients. Idaho Falls boasts a food scene that celebrates regional characteristics and delivers a great gastronomic experience.

As the afternoon unfolds, consider a visit to Melaleuca Field, the city's gorgeous ballpark. Even if there isn't a game scheduled during your visit, the field and the neighboring park offer a beautiful area for a stroll, relaxation, or a game of catch.

Adjacent to the ballpark, you'll find the Japanese Friendship Garden. This tranquil paradise gives a calm and meditative environment, complete with a koi pond, bridges, and gorgeous flora. It's a place to unwind and appreciate the quiet of the surroundings.

Afternoon activities can potentially include a float excursion down the Snake River. Snake River Float Trips provide an opportunity to explore the river's beauty and enjoy the quiet of the waterway.

As you float along the Snake River, you'll have the chance to take in the gorgeous scenery and feel the river's gentle bends. The peacefulness of the river creates a pleasant mood.

The Snake River and its riparian areas are home to different wildlife species, from bald eagles to moose. Keep a watch out for these occupants as you drift along.

The guides on the float trips often share cultural and historical insights about the river, its importance to the region, and the Native American tribes that have called it home.

Your day journey from Jackson Hole to Idaho Falls can, depending on you, culminate with a relaxing dinner in one of the city's restaurants. It's a chance to reflect on your journey and share your experiences with fellow travelers.

VI

Practical Information

23

Practical Ways To Stay Saved

While Jackson Hole offers unrivaled beauty and experiences, it's crucial to prioritize safety to make the most of your trip. Here, we'll present a thorough collection of safety guidelines targeted to the particular elements of Jackson Hole, helping you have a safe and pleasurable experience.

1. Respect Wildlife

Jackson Hole is home to a plethora of animals, including moose, elk, bears, and bison. While the opportunity to see these species in their natural habitat is a highlight of any visit, it's vital to do so responsibly:

- Keep a safe distance: Always maintain a respectful distance when witnessing wildlife. Use binoculars or a telephoto lens for close-ups.

- Do not feed animals: Feeding wildlife is not only harmful but also forbidden in national parks. Human feeding can hurt animals and change their natural behavior.

- Bear safety: If you're in bear area, make noise to notify bears of your presence, carry bear spray, and know how to use it. Hike in groups, as bears are less inclined to approach larger parties.

2. Weather Awareness
Jackson Hole's weather can be erratic, especially in the mountains. Here's how to keep safe:

- Check the weather: Before going on any outdoor activity, check the weather forecast. Sudden storms can be harmful on higher elevations.

- Dress in layers: The weather can change suddenly, so be prepared with layered clothing that can be altered as needed.

- Be prepared for altitude: Jackson Hole's high elevation can impact certain guests. Stay hydrated and avoid intense exercise until you've adapted.

3. Outdoor Adventure Safety
Outdoor sports including hiking, skiing, and rafting are prominent in Jackson Hole. Ensure your safety by:

- Inform someone of your plans: Before starting out on any outdoor trip, let someone know your itinerary and planned return time.

- Hiking safety: Stick to marked paths, carry essential supplies (water, first-aid kit, map, and compass), and be mindful of trail conditions.

- Ski and snowboard safety: If you're traveling in winter, be careful of avalanche danger, and ensure you're well-equipped with the right gear.

- Rafting safety: When participating in rafting expeditions, always wear a life jacket and obey the guide's instructions.

4. Wildlife Safety
   Wild creatures are a common sight in Jackson Hole, and it's crucial to know how to properly cohabit with them:

- Bison can be unpredictable and dangerous, so maintain a safe distance and never approach them.

- If you encounter a moose, stay your distance, since they can be aggressive when confronted.

- Be bear-aware: Familiarize yourself with bear safety recommendations and carry bear spray when exploring the environment.

5. Carry Essential Supplies
   Whether you're on a short hike or a full-day trip, it's vital to bring some basic supplies:

- Water: Stay hydrated, especially at higher heights.

- First-aid kit: Include bandages, antiseptic wipes, pain killers, and any necessary personal prescriptions.

- Map and compass or GPS: Knowing your location is vital, especially in rural locations.

- Whistle and signal mirror: These might be essential in situations.

6. Travel Safely on Mountain Roads

Many sights in Jackson Hole require traversing mountain roads. Follow these tips to guarantee a safe journey:

- Drive cautiously: Mountain roads can be steep and twisty. Reduce your speed and take additional caution on curves and switchbacks.

- Check road conditions: Be aware of any road closures or poor weather conditions that may influence your route.

- Use pull-outs: Pull over in designated spots to enable other vehicles to pass.

7. Respect Private Property

Jackson Hole is home to many private ranches and homes. Always respect property borders and do not trespass.

8. Water Safety

While enjoying the Snake River or other water bodies in the region, follow these guidelines:

- Wear life jackets: Whether you're rafting, kayaking, or simply swimming, wearing a life jacket is crucial for safety.

- Know your limits: Be mindful of your swimming ability and never take excessive risks.

9. Sun Protection
   The high elevation and bright skies in Jackson Hole ensure substantial solar exposure. Protect yourself from sunburn and UV radiation:

- Wear sunscreen: Use a broad-spectrum sunscreen with at least SPF 30.

- Wear sunglasses: Protect your eyes from intense sun glare.

- Wear a hat: A wide-brimmed hat provides additional protection for your face and neck.

10. Altitude Awareness
   Jackson Hole's elevation is substantially higher than many other sites, and some visitors may encounter symptoms of altitude sickness. Here's ways to lessen these effects:

- Hydrate: Drink plenty of water to help your body adjust to the altitude.

- Take it easy: Avoid vigorous activity in the first 24-48 hours to adapt.

- Recognize the signs: If you suffer symptoms like dizziness, nausea, or shortness of breath, descend to lower elevations.

11. Emergency Services and Contact

- For immediate emergencies, dial 911.

- Teton County Sheriff's Office (non-emergency): (307) 733-2331

- St. John's Health (for medical emergencies): (307) 733-3636

- Jackson Hole Mountain Resort Ski Patrol (for ski-related emergencies): (307) 733-2292

12. Follow Local Guidelines and Regulations
   Observe all rules, guidelines, and restrictions posted in national parks, nature reserves, and other public locations.

24

Local Ettiquette

J ackson Hole, Wyoming, is a unique place where the culture is as different as the environment. While its warm environment is clear, understanding and respecting local etiquette will enhance your experience as a first-time visitor or tourist. Here's a handbook to help you navigate the customs and values of this unique place.

1. Greet with Warmth: Jackson Hole inhabitants are recognized for their kind and inviting nature. When you meet someone, whether it's a local or another traveler, a grin and a warm "hello" go a long way. It's an area where strangers often begin up discussions, so don't be startled if someone starts chatting with you in the grocery store or on the hiking route.

2. Embrace the Western Spirit: The Western spirit is firmly embedded in Jackson Hole. You'll typically encounter people dressed in cowboy boots, jeans, and flannel shirts. Embrace the Western dress, and you'll feel like a local in no time. However, don't be surprised if you encounter a blend of Western attire

with high-end fashion – it's a unique Jackson Hole style.

3. Tipping Culture: Tipping is usual in Jackson Hole, as it is in most regions of the United States. In restaurants, pubs, and for services like guides and drivers, it's common to tip around 15-20% of the price. It's a method to show appreciation for exceptional service and is an important aspect of the local economy.

4. Respect Wildlife: The wildlife in Jackson Hole is one of the region's most prized assets. If you encounter wildlife, maintain a respectful distance and observe them from afar. Never approach or feed wild animals, and be cautious while driving, especially at dawn and dusk when animals are more active.

5. Leave No Trace: Jackson Hole's unspoiled wilderness is a treasure, and ethical outdoor ethics are crucial. Whether you're hiking, camping, or rafting, follow the "Leave No Trace" rules. This involves packing out all your waste, staying on designated trails, and preserving the environment to maintain its beauty for future generations.

6. Right of Way: On the hiking trails or when driving, the usual rule of thumb is that those heading upwards have the right of way. Always be respectful and give the trail to others when required.

7. Car Etiquette: In the small, attractive town of Jackson, traffic can get hectic, especially during peak tourist seasons. Be patient and considerate while driving. Don't block intersections, use

your turn signals, and respect the speed restrictions.

8. Quiet Hours: Many accommodations in Jackson Hole observe quiet hours, usually in the evening and early morning. This is to ensure a tranquil and relaxed environment for all guests. Be mindful of noise and observe these quiet hours, especially if you're staying in hotels or resorts.

9. No Smoking Zones: Jackson Hole has strict no-smoking zones in public locations, and many accommodations and outdoor areas are designated as smoke-free. Be mindful of these regulations and only smoke in approved areas.

10. Alcohol: Drinking in public areas is generally not allowed in Jackson Hole. While enjoying a drink at a restaurant or bar is common, public intoxication and disruptive behavior are not tolerated.

11. Cell Phone Usage: In many restaurants and social settings, the locals appreciate it if you keep your cell phone usage to a minimum. Engaging in conversation and enjoying the company of those around you is a cultural value in Jackson Hole.

12. Cowboy Code: Lastly, it's essential to embrace the Cowboy Code of ethics – honesty, integrity, respect, and courtesy. These values are deeply embedded in the community and respecting them will make your stay more enjoyable.

Jackson Hole welcomes visitors with open arms, and understanding and respecting these local etiquettes is not only polite but also a way to immerse yourself in the unique culture of the region. As you explore the stunning landscapes, embrace the Western spirit, and engage with the friendly locals, you'll find your Jackson Hole experience to be even more enriching and memorable.

VII

Sample Itineraries for Different Interests

25

Weekend Getaway

A weekend getaway in Jackson Hole promises a great blend of adventure, relaxation, and memorable experiences in the heart of the American West. Whether you're a nature enthusiast, an outdoor adventurer, or simply seeking a calm vacation, this itinerary delivers a sample of the best that Jackson Hole has to offer.

Day 1: Arrival and Downtown Exploration

Morning: - Arrive at Jackson Hole Airport or your selected means of transportation. Check into your accommodation, which can be a comfortable cabin, a boutique hotel, or a delightful bed & breakfast.

Lunch:
- Head to one of the downtown eateries for a wonderful lunch. Try local favorites like bison burgers or fish, or experience farm-to-table meals.

Afternoon: Downtown Exploration - Stroll through the streets of Jackson and discover the distinctive stores, art galleries, and boutiques. Don't miss to stop by the magnificent elk antler arches in Town Square.

Late Afternoon:

- Immerse yourself in art and nature at the National Museum of Wildlife Art, set on a hill with panoramic views. Explore the vast array of wildlife-inspired art.

Dinner:

- Enjoy a western-inspired meal at a neighborhood restaurant. Savor a steak or a hearty dinner accompanied with a wonderful range of wines.

Day 2: Outdoor Adventures and Scenic Beauty
Morning:

- Start your day with a leisurely breakfast at a neighborhood café. Fuel up for a day of outdoor activity.

Late Morning:

- Embark on a picturesque trip to Grand Teton National Park, where you'll be encircled by the towering peaks of the Teton Range. Hike one of the numerous picturesque paths, such Taggart Lake or Inspiration Point, and immerse yourself in the natural splendor.

Lunch:

- Enjoy a picnic lunch amidst the awe-inspiring views of Grand Teton National Park. There are designated picnic spaces and lovely spots to select from.

Afternoon:

- Join a guided Snake River float tour for a calm river journey. Drift along the Snake River, taking in the tranquil scenery and viewing wildlife.

Late Afternoon:

- Spend some time at Jackson Lake, where you can relax on the shore, enjoy a swim, or explore the lake by canoe or kayak.

Dinner:

- Savor a meal at a restaurant along the Snake River or in one of the nearby lodges. The sunset views over the water are spectacular.

Day 3: Wildlife Encounters and Cultural Exploration

Morning:

- Begin your day with a wildlife safari in the surrounding area. Join a guided tour to increase your chances of spotting local wildlife, including bison, elk, and possibly even bears.

Lunch:

- Stop for a casual lunch at a local café or diner. Enjoy classic American fare while discussing your wildlife sightings.

Afternoon:

- Visit the Jackson Hole Historical Society and Museum to learn about the region's history, culture, and the people who have shaped it.

Late Afternoon:

- Head to Teton Village and take the Aerial Tram to the summit of Rendezvous Mountain. The tram ride offers breathtaking views, and you can explore hiking trails or simply soak in the vistas.

Dinner:
- End your weekend getaway with dinner at a restaurant in Teton Village. Savor alpine-inspired dishes and toast to your memorable Jackson Hole experience.

Evening:
- Jackson Hole's low light pollution makes it an excellent place for stargazing. Join a local astronomy group or venture to a dark, open area for a night of celestial exploration.

Day 4: Departure

Morning:
- Enjoy your final breakfast in Jackson Hole. Depending on your departure time, you may have a bit of free time for last-minute shopping, exploring, or taking a scenic drive.

Departure:
- Depart from Jackson Hole with unforgettable memories of your weekend getaway in this spectacular destination. As you leave, you'll be taking a piece of the wild, wonderful West with you.

26

Family Vacation

A family vacation in Jackson Hole promises an exciting blend of outdoor thrills, wildlife encounters, and educational experiences. This program is designed to offer a memorable and fun-filled holiday for families of all ages.

Day 1: Arrival and Downtown Exploration

Morning:
   - Arrive at Jackson Hole Airport or your preferred means of transportation. Check into your family-friendly accommodation, which may include a cottage, resort, or vacation rental.

Lunch:
   - Enjoy lunch at a family-friendly restaurant in Jackson. Try the local pizza, burgers, or a classic American diner.

Afternoon: - Stroll through downtown Jackson with your family. Explore the distinctive stores, boutiques, and art galleries. Let the youngsters play in Town Square while you view the distinctive elk antler arches.

Late Afternoon: Jackson Hole Historical Society and Museum

- Visit the Jackson Hole Historical Society and Museum, where both adults and children may learn about the region's history and culture.

Dinner: Western Dining

- Indulge in a family evening at a restaurant that offers western-inspired cuisine. Sample local foods like bison chili or trout.

Day 2: Family Adventure in the Tetons

Morning:
   - Start your day with a substantial breakfast at a neighborhood café. Fuel up for a day of family adventure.

Late Morning:
   - Head to Grand Teton National Park, where your family may discover the natural splendor of the Teton Range. Take a gentle hike on routes ideal for all ages, such as Taggart Lake or Bradley Lake.

Lunch:
   - Have a picnic lunch in the park. Many designated places offer picturesque spots to enjoy a family dinner amidst stunning surroundings.

Afternoon:

- Explore Jenny Lake, where your family can enjoy a boat ride across the lake to Hidden Falls and Inspiration Point. The boat ride provides an element of adventure and the possibility to view wildlife.

Late Afternoon: - Return to Jackson and spend some time swimming and resting at your accommodation's pool or a local swimming hole. It's an opportunity for both youngsters and adults to decompress.

Dinner:
  - Dine at a family-friendly restaurant in Jackson. Choose a place with a menu that appeals to youngsters and adults alike.

Day 3: Wildlife Encounters and Outdoor Fun

Morning:
  - Start your day with a guided wildlife safari. It's an opportunity for the whole family to view bison, elk, and other creatures in their natural habitat.

Lunch:
  - Enjoy lunch at a local café or diner. Satisfy your hunger with classic American comfort cuisine.

Afternoon:
  - Join a family-friendly guided Snake River float tour. It's a time for everyone to mingle and take in the tranquil river surroundings. Be on the watch for wildlife near the riverbanks.

Late Afternoon:

- Jackson Hole includes family adventure parks where you may do activities like zip-lining, climbing walls, and bungee trampolines. Kids and adults can enjoy these amazing trips together.

Dinner:
- Opt for casual meals at a local restaurant or pizzeria. Let the youngsters choose their favorite dishes.

Day 4: Fun and Learning

Morning:
- Enjoy breakfast at your accommodation. Afterwards, visit a nearby animal refuge or petting zoo where the kids may get up close to creatures like elk, deer, or even bison.

Lunch:
- Have a family picnic along the banks of the Snake River. It's a great location for a relaxing supper.

Afternoon: - Explore the National Museum of Wildlife Art, which offers family-friendly exhibits and educational programs. Kids can engage with interactive displays and art.

Late Afternoon:
- Take the Aerial Tram to the summit of Rendezvous Mountain in Teton Village. The tram ride provides exhilarating views and an opportunity to explore the paths and admire the surroundings.

Dinner:

- Celebrate your last evening in Jackson Hole with a special dinner at a family-friendly restaurant in Teton Village. Savor a dinner that everyone can enjoy.

Day 5: Departure

Morning:

- Enjoy breakfast at your accommodation and take some time for a final walk or tour in Jackson Hole.

Departure:
- Depart from Jackson Hole with cherished family memories of your fantastic trip in this intriguing section of Wyoming. As you depart, you'll be carrying with you a piece of the wild, amazing West.

27

Outdoor Enthusiast

Day 1: Arrival at Grand Teton National Park

Morning: - Arrive at Jackson Hole Airport or your selected means of transportation. Check into your accommodation, which might be a cabin, lodge, or camping for a truly outdoor experience.

Lunch: - Enjoy a substantial local lunch at a restaurant in Jackson. Fuel yourself for your adventure-filled voyage.

Afternoon: - Head to Grand Teton National Park, where you'll encounter the beautiful Teton Range. Start with a hike on a popular trail like Jenny Lake, Taggart Lake, or Cascade Canyon.

Dinner: - Embrace the outdoors atmosphere and make a campfire supper at your campsite or lodge. Savor the taste of a dinner amid the outdoors.

Day 2: Hiking and Wildlife Encounters

Morning: - Start your day with breakfast surrounded by the natural splendor of Jackson Hole. Consider a campground breakfast or dine at a local café.

Late Morning: - Continue your trekking exploration in Grand Teton National Park. Venture on routes like Delta Lake, Paintbrush Canyon, or Death Canyon to take in different facets of the park.

Lunch:

- Enjoy a picnic lunch in the midst of the park. Find a lovely area with views of the towering peaks for your meal.

Afternoon:

- Join a guided wildlife excursion to observe iconic animals including moose, elk, and bison. Knowledgeable guides will enhance your wildlife viewing experience.

Dinner: - Dine at a local restaurant in Jackson or Teton Village to sample local recipes that emphasize area ingredients.

Day 3: Thrilling Adventures

Morning:

- Have a short breakfast to fuel up for a day of exploration.

Late Morning:

- Embark on an adrenaline-pumping whitewater rafting experience on the Snake River. Jackson Hole features spectacular Class III and IV rapids.

Lunch:

- Enjoy a packed lunch along the riverbank or opt for the food served during your rafting adventure.

Afternoon:

- For a soaring adventure, enjoy paragliding or zip-lining in Teton Village. These activities provide a unique view on the landscape.

Dinner:

- After a day of high-energy activities, enjoy a quiet dinner at a neighborhood restaurant. Sample regional beers and unwind.

Day 4: Outdoor Excursions and Relaxation

Morning:

- Take a day excursion to the Shoshone National Forest, just east of Yellowstone. Hike, bike, or explore this unspoiled wilderness.

Lunch:

- Pack a picnic for a pleasant outdoor lunch amidst the forest's quiet surroundings.

Afternoon: - Try your hand at fly fishing in the Snake River or go for a magnificent horseback ride in the countryside.

Dinner:

- Conclude your day with a scenic BBQ meal at your accommodation or a local place with mountain views.

Day 5: Grand Finale

Morning:

  - Start early for a sunrise hike in Grand Teton National Park. The beautiful morning light on the peaks is a magical sight.

Lunch:

  - Dine at a café in Teton Village, tasting alpine-inspired food while you reflect on your journey.

Afternoon:

  - Take the Aerial Tram to Rendezvous Mountain for magnificent views of the Tetons. Hike, rest, or soak in the magnificence of the countryside.

Dinner:

  - Enjoy a memorable meal at a restaurant in Teton Village, marking the end of your wonderful outdoor trip.

Evening:

  - Cap off your visit with stargazing in the dark skies of Jackson Hole. Join an astronomy group or simply lie back and stare at the stars.

Day 6: Departure

Morning: - Enjoy a leisurely breakfast and cherish your final moments in Jackson Hole. Take a lovely drive or a short trek if time allows.

Departure: - Depart from Jackson Hole, but carry with you the memories of an unforgettable outdoor trip in one of the most beautiful places in the world.

This itinerary offers a thrilling and nature-focused adventure for outdoor enthusiasts, showcasing the finest of Jackson Hole's natural wonders, exhilarating activities, and quiet scenery. Whether you're hiking, rafting, or simply enjoying the grandeur of the Tetons, you'll leave Jackson Hole with a greater connection to the wild, untamed beauty of the region.

28

Romantic Retreat

Day 1: Arrival and Romantic Welcome
  Morning: - Arrive at Jackson Hole Airport or your selected means of transportation. Check into a romantic, intimate accommodation, whether it's a tiny cabin, a boutique lodge, or a magnificent resort.

Lunch: - Begin your retreat with lunch at a nearby restaurant where you can enjoy regional favorites like bison, elk, or trout.

Afternoon: - Rejuvenate with a couple's massage at a spa or wellness center in Jackson Hole. It's the perfect way to start your romantic holiday.

Supper: - Enjoy a romantic supper at an upmarket restaurant in Jackson. Savor delicious meals and great wines as you toast to the beginning of your romantic retreat.

Day 2: Exploration and Adventure

Morning: - Start your day with a leisurely breakfast in your accommodation. Many locations provide breakfast in bed or private dining alternatives.

Late Morning: - Head to Grand Teton National Park to experience the stunning landscapes. Stroll hand in hand along Jenny Lake or take a scenic drive to admire the vistas of the Teton Range.

Lunch: - Have a picnic lunch in the park with a basket of gourmet delights. Find a peaceful area with serene views to share a lunch.

Afternoon: - Experience the thrill of a private wildlife safari where you can spot moose, elk, and bison in a remote setting. It's a chance to connect with nature and each other.

Dinner: - Dine at a restaurant with a deck overlooking the mountains. Enjoy the beautiful sunset views as you relish a romantic dinner for two.

Day 3: Serene and Scenic

Morning: - Enjoy a sumptuous breakfast at a ranch, surrounded by the splendor of the Wyoming countryside. Savor fresh farm-to-table ingredients.

Late Morning: - Take a lovely drive to Jackson Lake, where you may enjoy a calm morning by the water. Rent a canoe or kayak for a serene paddle together.

meal: - Have a lakeside meal at a wonderful restaurant or opt for a picnic by the sea. The calm of the lake creates an intimate setting.

Afternoon: - Embark on a private boat tour on Jackson Lake, where you may discover hidden coves and have the lake to yourselves.

Dinner: - Dine in an intimate restaurant tucked away in the forests or mountains. Many places in Jackson Hole provide private dinner experiences for couples.

Day 4: Adventure and Connection

Morning: - Start your day with a thrilling experience, whether it's horseback riding, hiking, or paragliding. Bond through a shared adrenaline sensation.

Lunch: - Enjoy a hilltop picnic with panoramic views. Savor the delicacies of the region while feeling on top of the world.

Afternoon: - Spend the afternoon at a spa center, hot spring, or in a calm area in the woods, reconnecting and unwinding together.

Dinner: - Dine at a restaurant that has a large wine list. Savor a romantic meal combined with exquisite wines to make a memorable evening.

Day 5: Farewell and Reflection

Morning: - Enjoy a leisurely breakfast and take a little walk to spend your last minutes in Jackson Hole.

Departure: - Depart from Jackson Hole, but take with you the cherished memories of a romantic getaway that reinforced your bond amidst the magnificence of the Tetons.

This romantic retreat program offers the perfect blend of leisure, adventure, and intimacy, providing an unforgettable experience for you and your loved one amid the beautiful surroundings of Jackson Hole, Wyoming. Whether you're sharing a private wildlife safari, a secluded lakeside lunch, or a thrilling adventure, you'll leave Jackson Hole with your bond stronger than ever.